The GREATEST
in the WORLD

illustrated by
Peter Bellingham

Peter Osborne

The Greatest

Cookery

Tips in the World

A 'The Greatest in the World' Book

www.thegreatestintheworld.com

Illustrations:
Peter Belllingham
www.peterbellinghamillustration.co.uk

Cover & layout design:
The designcouch
www.designcouch.co.uk

Cover images: © Clive Nichols; © Igor Dutina;
© Kyryl Rudenko; © Rohit Seth; © Andzej Tokarski
courtesy of www.fotolia.com

Copy editor: Bronwyn Robertson
www.theartsva.com

Series creator/editor: Steve Brookes

First edition published in 2006 by Public Eye Publications

This edition published in 2007
by The Greatest in the World Ltd, PO Box 3182,
Stratford-upon-Avon, Warwickshire CV37 7XW

Text and Illustrations Copyright © 2007 – The Greatest in the World Ltd.

A CIP catalogue record for this book is available from the British Library
ISBN 978-1-905151-64-6

Printed and bound in China by 1010 Printing International Ltd.

I would like to dedicate this book to my family.

First of all to my Dad, sadly no longer with us, who never saw this part of my life but has inspired me in so many ways. Hope you are watching, Dad!

Then to the four women in my life. My Mum, who watches and listens to every show; my lovely wife Anna-Marie; our beautiful daughter Amelia and not forgetting our cat, Puss Puss, who is probably the best fed cat in the neighbourhood!

Thank you all for your love, help and support over the years.

I would also like to thank Christine for taking time out of her busy life to write the foreword to this book. She really is a remarkable lady and a lovely friend.

I hope you all enjoy the book!

Contents

Foreword

Peter Osborne burst into my life when I interviewed him at 'The Ideal Home Show' for a radio show which Neil and I were presenting. He steamed into the studio looking like a large exotic, fruit meringue on legs wearing a white chef's jacket and multi-coloured trousers. It was immediately obvious he is devoted not only to cooking but also to eating! I entirely endorse Peter's maxim: "Never trust a thin chef". If portion size, in the person of the chef, is any guide to culinary ability, then Peter is exceptionally well-endowed!

During our interview (and, indeed, ever since) I have profited from Peter's wealth of hints and tips gathered over many years. He is always willing to share his expertise, in a witty yet easily-understood way, with TV viewers, radio listeners and audiences at his live shows. In fact with anyone who will listen and let's be honest – he loves talking!

When Granada TV asked Neil and me to take over a restaurant for a day and cook for some unsuspecting punters, my instinctive reaction was to ring Peter for advice. Cooking against the clock with inadequate facilities (well, Neil can hardly boil water without expert help!) needed every ounce of Peter's wit and wisdom. He surpassed himself and, with his help, so did we.

At last, Peter has whipped up his best tips into a gourmet confection and here they are for your delectation. Good cooks are not necessarily able to impart their expertise. Peter's advice is simple but practical and I promise you there is no 'gobbledy-cook'. Not only will his tips make your life and your cooking easier, they will save you time and money as well.

However clever you may be, however accomplished in the kitchen, you cannot live without this book!

Christine

X

Cooking is like making love, you do it well, or you do not do it at all.

Marleen Harriet van Horne

Useful cookery tips

section 1
Useful cookery tips

Fresh eggs

To check the freshness of an egg, dissolve 30ml (2 tablespoons) of salt in about 268ml (1 pint) of water. Place the egg in the water. If the egg sinks then it is fresh, if it floats then it is stale.

Ripe melons

To check the ripeness of a melon, hold it firmly in both hands and lightly press around the end of the melon, opposite the stem. The surface should give slightly under the pressure. A ripe melon will also have a pleasant sweet smell.

Quick tip

EGG TEMPERATURE
Eggs should be brought to room temperature before use, so if you do keep them in the fridge, try to remember to take them out an hour before using.

Size your vegetables

When buying vegetables such as Brussels sprouts try to choose all the same size so that they all cook at an even rate. If you are hosting an important dinner party similar sized vegetables look much nicer on the plate!

Fresh beans

To check the freshness of a runner bean, hold it between your forefinger and thumb and bend it gently. If it is fresh it will break in two rather than bend.

Frozen wine cubes

Never throw away any unused wine left after parties. It can easily be frozen in ice cube trays and then dropped into soups and sauces as required.

Storing an iced cake

Store an iced cake on the lid of a cake tin, with the inverted tin over it. You can then slice and remove pieces without risking damage trying to take the cake out of the tin.

Quick tip

RESCUING OVER-SALTED COOKING

Over-salted vegetables, casseroles or other dishes can be saved by dropping a peeled, cut potato into the water. Simmer until the potato is soft then carefully lift it out. The potato should have absorbed a lot of the saltiness.

You can also disguise saltiness by adding a small can of tomatoes, a dash of sweet sherry or a little plain yoghurt, whichever is most suitable for the particular dish involved.

Longer-lasting fruit cake

To improve the life of a large fruit cake cut It in half, take slices from the middle of the cake and then slide the two halves back together. Store the cake in an airtight container.

Flour shaker

To make a home made flour shaker, make several holes in the metal lid of a screw top jar by hammering a nail through it while resting it on a wooden board. Fill the jar with flour and replace the lid.

Non-stick honey

To measure honey and syrups easily, use a metal spoon that has been dipped in hot water. Honey and syrups will not stick to the heated spoon.

Stain removal

Amazingly a potato will take food stains off your fingers. Just slice and rub the raw potato on the stains and then rinse with water.

Making chopped tomatoes

Canned chopped tomatoes are more expensive than whole ones. Save money by buying cans of whole ones and chopping them up, whilst still in the can, with a pair of scissors.

Freezing tomatoes

If you find yourself with an abundance of tomatoes from your garden at the end of the growing season (or great prices at the farmers' market or 'pick your own') try freezing them. They will not be suitable for slicing, but their flavour will be better than canned tomatoes when used in soups, stews or sauces. Remove the stems and, after rinsing and drying, place them whole in a plastic freezer bag. You can also chop them and puree them in a food processor before freezing the thick liquid. Add some fresh chopped basil to a few of the bags for ready to cook Italian-style sauce bases.

When you need whole tomatoes for cooking simply run a frozen one under the tap for a few seconds and slide off the skin. They can be sliced while frozen and are also quick and easy to deseed when half thawed. Remember that, once frozen, tomatoes can only be used for cooking purposes; they are not suitable for salads.

An alternative way to freeze tomatoes is to remove the stem top, cut the tomatoes in half and place, cut side up, in a roasting pan. Drizzle them with a little oil. Roast uncovered at 150°C/300°F/gas 6 for 2 hours. Allow them to cool, place in plastic bags and freeze. They will be great in winter soups, stews, casseroles, pasta sauces and chilli.

Grape tips

Before buying grapes you should shake the bunch gently, if grapes fall off the bunch is not fresh. To store grapes, wrap loosely in newspaper and keep in the dark.

Useful dried herbs and spices

Keeping your herbs and spices cabinet well stocked is the key to easier cooking and baking. In addition to salt and black pepper, the following should always be in your cupboard:

Dried Basil	Garlic Powder
Dried Parsley	Chilli Powder
Ground Cinnamon	Dill
Ground Ginger	Dried Oregano
Paprika	Dried Rosemary
Dried Thyme	Vanilla Extract

Quick tip

JUICY CITRUS
Citrus fruits such as lemons and oranges, should feel heavy for their size if they are full of juice. They will also yield most juice if they are stored at room temperature. If they have been stored in a fridge, microwave each one for about 4 seconds to increase the amount of juice produced.

Cutting for success

Cutting foods into a uniform size and shape is important to the success of a recipe as it allows the ingredients to cook at the same rate. If you add some carrots to a soup that are 6mm (¼ inch) thick and some that are 25mm (1") thick you can expect an uneven result as one will either be overcooked or undercooked.

Simple cake decoration

A fast and effective way to finish a cake requires only a paper lace-type doily and powdered sugar (or cocoa powder). Simply centre the doily on top of the cake and sprinkle on a light, even layer of icing sugar or cocoa. Carefully lift the doily off the cake (straight up) and you should be left with an attractive design.

CURRY TOO HOT?
If your curry turns out to be too hot, add a carton of plain yoghurt or sour cream to take the edge off the heat.

Good quality cabbage

Before buying a cabbage, check that the heart is firm by pressing the centre with your thumb.

Homemade mini icing bags

To make small icing bags, take a freezer bag and place the icing inside. Close the bag and snip a small hole in one corner. It is essential to use freezer quality bags as the sandwich ones are not strong enough and will burst when you try to squeeze out the icing.

Wrapping butter

Always wrap butter well before you store it in the fridge as it easily picks up odours from any strong foods kept near it.

Care with spices

Don't measure or shake spices over open boiling saucepans, as you may drop too much into the pan. Also the steam might enter the jar, causing the spice grains to stick together in lumps and therefore spoil.

Mirrored service

For that important or special party, use a mirror tile from which to serve canapés instead of a plate. These can be bought relatively cheaply from a DIY store.

Washing lettuce

Leafy lettuces should always be washed thoroughly before using. Fill a large bowl with cold water, separate the leaves and swirl them in the water. Allow them to sit in the bowl for a short time. If there is an excessive amount of dirt in the bottom of the bowl then repeat the process. Always dry the leaves before using, either in a salad spinner or by patting gently with a towel.

Chopsticks

Using chopsticks can be a fun way to break your daily dining routine. Many dieters find that they eat less because the pace of eating is slowed, especially when just learning to use them! The same slowing down of eating and ingesting smaller mouthfuls also aids digestion.

No more bubbling jam

To stop jam bubbling out of jam tarts before the pastry is cooked, keep the jam in the fridge before use – simple but very effective.

Cracking a coconut

This is the most efficient way to crack a coconut: puncture one of its 'eyes' with an ice pick or the tip of a sharp knife. Pour out the milk and save it. Then crack the coconut by hitting it with a hammer in the middle, where the shell is widest. Continue cracking around the nut until you have made a circle and can separate the two halves. Finally prise the coconut out of the shell. To shred it, remove the coconut flesh from the hard shell, along with the brown papery inner covering, and rub the coconut 'meat' against a food grater.

Yeast 'use by' dates

It is important to check the date of expiration on yeast before adding it to a recipe. Yeast is a living ingredient and won't perform correctly if it is past its prime. It is especially important for the casual baker to check the date to avoid wasting a lot of time and ingredients.

Freezer labelling

Have you ever found a package of food in your freezer and asked yourself "What IS this?". You can avoid this dilemma simply by labelling each freezer bag with a permanent marker. Also remember that food does not keep indefinitely after freezing, so add the date of freezing to the label and check your frozen items at least once every month.

Choosing a pear

Pears are one of the only fruits that ripen better off the tree rather than on it. The best-tasting pears are those that are picked immature and allowed to ripen in storage or even on the grocer's shelf. Choose brightly coloured pears; avoid cut, shrivelled, or bruised pears, as they are likely to be bruised inside.

No nutcracker?

To crack nuts without a nutcracker, use either a pair of pliers or mole grips. With the nut held in place, wrap the whole thing in a tea towel before you apply pressure, which will avoid the bits going everywhere.

Clogged garlic press

To clean out a clogged-up garlic press, use a toothbrush. Preferably an old one!

Dry beans

Always soak dry beans before cooking them. It makes them more easily digestible. It also makes them cook more quickly. Cover the beans with cold water and allow them to soak overnight. Remember to change the water a few times and rinse the beans thoroughly before cooking. Alternatively you can use the "quick method" – bring to a boil, cook for 3 minutes, cover and allow to rest 1 hour. Finally there is a third possibility if you are in a hurry. Simply add the dry beans at the beginning of the recipe. You will have to allow for additional cooking time which can range from 30– 60 minutes, depending on the type of bean.

Quick tip

RESCUING LUMPY GRAVY

Lumpy gravy can be rescued! The usual cause is improper combining of liquid with roux (a mixture of flour and fat used to thicken). Simply strain the gravy through a fine mesh strainer or colander. Discard any lumps and continue to simmer the gravy until the desired thickness is reached.

Storing onions and garlic

Onions and garlic are best stored hung in strings so there is a good circulation of air to avoid disease spores causing mould. Most of us don't get time to do this properly these days so a great alternative is to put the onions or garlic in a nylon stocking, and tie a knot between each one to prevent them from touching. When you require an onion or garlic bulb then simply cut off just below a knot.

Take good care of your chocolate

To maintain the quality of chocolate, store it wrapped in a cool dry place. If it becomes too warm or damp, some changes in flavour and texture may occur. Never refrigerate fine chocolate. It is best to use chocolate within six months of purchase – if it lasts that long!

Need to use half an egg?

Although most recipes list the number of whole eggs to use, it can be useful to know a conversion measurement. This can come in handy if you want to make only half of a particular recipe. The average large egg is about 57g (4 tablespoons). Simply lightly whip the egg and measure the required fraction.

Easy-slice corned beef

Storing tinned corned beef in the fridge will make it much easier to slice when required.

No matches?

If you have candles to light and no matches or lighter in your house, light one end of a long piece of dried spaghetti on the gas hob and use this as a taper.

Sticky lids

Before resealing a jar or bottle of sticky food, wipe the rim and lid with a paper towel that has been dampened with hot water; this will prevent the lid from getting sticky.

Shopping list

Always keep a current shopping list on view in the kitchen – maybe attached to the refrigerator door with a magnet. Each time you use up an item of food, add it to the list. When you go shopping, take a bulldog clip or clothes peg with you to attach your shopping list to the trolley so that it doesn't get lost.

Shopping with children

When you can't avoid taking the children along shopping for food, try incorporating them in the task. Divide up your list and let the youngsters help find the items for you. For little ones who already know how to count it can be an experience in counting or a form of language development and learning, as they discover the names of their favourite foods.

Storing hard cheese

Keep hard cheeses such as mature Cheddar or Parmesan moist during storage by wrapping in a clean piece of cloth that has been dampened with beer. Keep in an airtight container in a refrigerator for one to two weeks.

Quick tip

OPENING AN OVEN

When opening oven doors, open the door a little at first, to allow the initial surge of heat and any steam from food being cooked to be released, and then open the door completely. Before opening it move your body away from the opening, and make sure you are not bent over with your head or any other part of your body directly above or near the opening.

Non-slip worktop

To stop a chopping board or bowl from moving on a kitchen worktop during use, place a damp tea-towel underneath first.

Get the defrosting bug!

Get into the habit of defrosting the fridge and freezer regularly, unless they do this automatically or are 'frost-free'. This helps to make sure that they are working properly and efficiently, so that the food inside is stored correctly and safely.

Bacteria-free sponges

To disinfect and kill bacteria in kitchen sponges (the cleaning variety – not the cake!) wash the sponge thoroughly, and then microwave it, while it is wet, for approx. 30 to 40 seconds on high. Watch carefully and when you see steam from the sponge, the bacteria in the sponge will be dead and you can stop the microwave. Remove the sponge carefully as it will be very hot! When cool, wash the sponge thoroughly before use. Never use this tip with a sponge that has any metal components.

Slicing bread

Improper slicing can ruin a beautiful homemade or bakery loaf of bread. Always slice fresh bread using a proper bread knife with a serrated blade. For best results remember to use a 'sawing' motion and press downward as little as possible. Let the knife do the work! Keep the top of the knife perpendicular to the loaf to ensure even slices. Always allow freshly-baked bread to cool on a rack before attempting to cut it.

Kitchen safety

Whilst cooking can be satisfying and enjoyable, it can also be disastrous if safety is not observed. The following tips for kitchen safety might appear obvious, however it can be so easy to forget for a moment, especially when children are helping out ...

- Avoid leaving food that is cooking unattended for a long period of time, if at all. If using a timer, have it with you at all times to remind you that you have something brewing in the kitchen.

- Turn handles of pots and pans inward and not sticking out.

- Avoid reaching over the stovetop when cooking and watch your sleeves − especially over a gas hob.

- Keep curtains, potholders, towels, and any other combustibles away from cooking areas.

- Do not put knives or other sharp objects into a full sink. Someone could reach in and accidentally get hurt.

- Never store sharp knives in drawers with other kitchen utensils. It is too easy to forget they are there when searching for something in a hurry.

- When processing hot liquids in a blender (such as sauces and soups), make sure the blender's lid is back on, then cover the lid with a towel and your hand, before proceeding to blend. Also, do not fill the blender more than halfway.

- Wash your dishcloths, towels and sponges frequently to get rid of bacteria or simply replace them more often.

- Keep children and pets away from appliances when cooking.

- Keep appliance cords as short as possible to avoid accidents such as tripping or knocking the appliance over.

- Have a small fire extinguisher and a first aid kit readily accessible in the kitchen. Also make sure that smoke detectors are fitted throughout your house – not just one at the bottom of the stairs.

Burnt-on food

To remove burnt-on food from a glass dish simply fill it with hot water, drop in a denture cleaning tablet and leave overnight. The next morning rinse well to leave a sparkling dish!

Flour sieve

To evenly flour a work surface before working with pastry, sprinkle the flour through a sieve.

Quick tip

SWEAT-FREE CHEESE

When you buy cheese wrapped in plastic, remove the wrapping as soon as you get home. Then wrap the cheese tightly in greaseproof paper, this will stop it from sweating and it will keep for longer.

Freezing bananas

Banana skins become flecked when ripe and it's best to eat the fruit at this stage. If you are worried about bananas becoming over-ripe or if you find yourself with an over-abundance, try freezing them for later cooking uses. Wrapped in clingfilm, still in their skins, they will keep in the freezer for up to six months. Eat them while still slightly frozen, or mash them and use in drinks or baking. Don't worry if the peel darkens during freezing as the fruit inside will still be pale. As with most foods, freezing changes the texture of bananas so they are best used in recipes like breads, pies, puddings, cakes, and ice cream. Use them within four to six months of freezing.

Soften hard sugar

If you have a dish or bag of hardened brown sugar, place a slice of apple in it to soften it again.

Quick tip

EASY-PEEL SHALLOTS
Shallots are peeled more easily when you pour boiling water over them.

Butter frying

When frying with butter, prevent it from burning by adding a little cooking oil as it melts.

Perky mash

To revive lifeless mashed potatoes, just whisk an egg white until stiff and fold carefully into the potatoes. Put the mixture into a dish and bake in a hot oven until fluffy and golden.

Ripening tomatoes

Tomatoes that are picked or purchased before they are ripe can be made ready for use in your kitchen. Contrary to popular belief, sunlight does not ripen a picked tomato (it will cause it to firm up, not truly ripen). Gentle heat will cause the tomatoes to ripen. Place them in a warm area of your kitchen (near your stove) and check them often.

To ripen tomatoes quickly, place them in a paper bag with an apple. Leave in a cool dark place and the tomatoes will ripen in a couple of days. As the apple ripens, it gives off a gas called ethylene which speeds up the ripening of the tomatoes. A banana will do a similar job but the strong smell may taint the tomato.

Peeling hard-boiled eggs

The shells of hard-boiled eggs are easy to remove if done so while the eggs are still slightly warm from cooking. Refrigerating them with the shells on tends to bind the outer covering to the cooked egg. Briefly cool the eggs in running water after cooking. Peel, cover and store them in the refrigerator until needed. They should keep well for two to three days.

Sharpening mug!

If you don't have a steel to sharpen your knives use the base of an unglazed earthenware mug. Run the blade across it at a slight angle. Do this several times in the same direction and then turn over to do the other side.

Quick tip

FRESH CAKE AND BISCUITS
To always ensure that your baked goods stay fresh and last longer put a small piece of bread inside your biscuit jar, cake tin, etc.

Grilling in an oven

When grilling in an oven always leave the oven door open. If the door remains closed the air cannot circulate and you end up baking the food rather than grilling it!

Food glazing

Brushing foods with products like marmalades or jellies is a simple way to add flavour during the last few minutes of broiling. Chicken and pork are especially good when paired with fruit glazes. Chicken goes well with apricot jelly or lemon marmalade and try pork with redcurrant jelly, Jalapeño jelly or orange marmalade. Preserves and maple syrup can also help create interesting new flavours. Remember that all these products have high sugar content and can quickly burn.

Filling without a funnel

To fill jars without spills, if you don't have a funnel, improvise by using a washing up liquid bottle. Remove the lid and cut off the base of the bottle. Wash and dry thoroughly before use.

Get the best from herbs

Get the most out of fresh herbs by adding them to a recipe at the ideal time. The flavour of tough-leaved herbs like rosemary, thyme or sage benefit from long cooking times. Add these herbs near the beginning of a preparation. The more delicate varieties such as basil, parsley and tarragon respond best to short simmering. Add them near the end of the recipe.

Peeling tomatoes

Recipes sometimes call for peeled fresh tomatoes. This can easily be done by dropping the whole tomato in boiling water for five seconds. Carefully remove the tomato and then drop immediately into cold water. The skin should be then be split, making it easy to peel off.

Buying chillies

When you are purchasing varieties of hot chillies you are not familiar with, as a general rule of thumb, the smaller the size of the top of the chilli, the hotter the flavour will be.

Sprouting potatoes

To prevent potatoes from sprouting when stored, place an apple amongst them.

Roasting garlic

Roasted garlic adds a rich full flavour to dressings, sauces, and marinades and can be prepared easily at home. The supermarket bought varieties tend to have lost a lot of their flavour by the time they are purchased so try home-grown cloves or those bought from independent greengrocers. Pre-heat your oven to 325°C/150°C/gas 4. Toss about 10 cloves (skin on) with 2 tablespoons of olive oil. Place in a roasting pan, sprinkle on a little water and season with salt and pepper. Place on a baking tray, loosely cover with foil and cook for about 45 minutes. Cool slightly and squeeze the garlic from its skin into a small bowl. If not using immediately, place in a covered container and refrigerate until needed.

Richer pot roast

A simple way to enrich the gravy for a pot roast is to make a rich roux. Melt 2 tablespoons of butter in a saucepan, whisk in 4 tablespoons of flour and cook for 5 minutes, stirring frequently. Set this aside. After your roast has been cooking for ¾ of its designated cooking time, carefully drain off all but 1 cup of the liquid from the roasting dish into the saucepan with the flour and butter mix. Cook for 5 minutes, stirring often. Pour the mixture over the roast, cover and complete the cooking time.

The cooked cake test

A cocktail stick or toothpick can be used to test whether a cake is ready; if it comes out clean then the cake is ready.

Sugar substitute

Add a much richer flavour in baking recipes by substituting honey or golden syrup for granulated sugar. For 100g (3½ oz) of sugar simply replace with 200g (7oz) of honey. Remember that honey and syrup contain about 20% water so you might need to reduce the liquid content of some recipes accordingly. Try using half honey and half sugar in bread recipes.

Cool pastry

To keep your pastry cool and easy to handle, instead of using a rolling pin use a straight sided, corked wine bottle and fill with chilled water. Chill the bottle first if necessary.

Quick tip

LIGHTER SCRAMBLED EGG
Add a small amount of water to your eggs before whipping them for scrambling. This produces steam during cooking and makes for a lighter finished product. Avoid adding milk, as it tends to make the eggs tough.

Add flavour to your barbeque

A great way to add flavour when barbequing is to smoke with fresh herbs. Choose medium-sized bunches of rosemary or thyme and soak them in water for at least 15 minutes. Shake off the excess water and place them directly on the hot coals. Replace the grill and add the food immediately. This method works really well with pork, chicken, or lamb.

Storing vegetables

Take potatoes, carrots etc. out of the supermarket plastic bags as soon as you get home. This will stop them sweating and they will stay fresh for longer.

Boiling eggs

When boiling eggs, prevent the shells from cracking by adding a pinch of salt to the water first. If eggshells do crack during boiling add a little vinegar to the water. This will set the white and prevent any further egg white or yolk from leaking out.

To prevent black rings from forming around the yolks of hard-boiled eggs, drain them as soon as they are cooked and crack the shells under cold running water to cool quickly.

Quick tip

NO CASTER SUGAR?

To make caster sugar from granulated sugar, place the granulated sugar into a food processor with a metal blade and whizz for a few seconds to get the right consistency.

Chilli too hot?

If you have made Chilli con Carne that is too hot and spicy, add a dollop of mayonnaise and stir in well. This will cool down the dish.

Choosing a coconut

Canned coconut milk works nicely enough for most recipes, but there is nothing like the taste of the milk fresh from the nut. When choosing one, look for a coconut that is heavy for its size. You should be able to hear the liquid sloshing around when you shake it; if you don't, the coconut has dried out.

Quick tip

DRYING HERBS

When drying herbs use the clean bags provided with the tablets for washing machines. Put in the fresh herbs and hang them to dry. When they are ready just rub the bags between your hands onto a piece of paper and then store the dried herbs that fall out of them in empty jars. All the herb stems will be left in the bags making it a very quick and easy method.

Keep an eye on mussels

Discard any mussels that are open before cooking or closed after cooking.

Flavoursome gravy

Use the vegetable water from boiled vegetables when making gravy. This way you get more flavour and won't waste the goodness that has come out of the vegetables into the water.

The wonder of bay

Bay leaves are an indispensable ingredient in the kitchen and add flavour to many soups, stocks and stews. They are the basis of the French 'bouquet garni'. This is a mixture of bay and several additional herbs tied together in cheesecloth, then dropped into a simmering pot. Bay leaves are especially good as flavourings for various savoury, carbohydrate dishes such as potato casseroles, bean stews and risotto. Most modern recipes suggest that the bay leaf is removed before serving the dish, as it can potentially cause someone to choke. Always use the leaves sparingly or they will make a dish too bitter.

In the past many traditions grew up around the fate of the person who found a bay leaf in their bowl. Many families rewarded the finder with extra dessert. Some believed that the person was entitled to a wish. However, others assigned the task of washing the dishes or clearing the table to the recipient of the bay leaf!

Quick tip

HOMEMADE SELF-RAISING FLOUR
If you run out of self-raising flour, the general rule for making your own is 2½ teaspoons of baking powder to 225g (8oz) of plain flour.

Garlic oil

Garlic that cooks to the point of browning can add a bitter taste to a dish. Always add the garlic to hot oil near the end of the cooking process. An alternative method is to cook with garlic-infused oil. Simply warm the oil over medium heat, remove from the flame and add the fresh chopped garlic. Allow to steep. Strain and use when preparing recipes calling for garlic. Use about 1 teaspoon of garlic to 150ml (¼ pint) of water.

Freezing cheese

Only freeze cheese containing more than 45% fat. Cheese with a lower fat content will separate and become grainy when frozen. Previously frozen cheeses are best used in cooking (sauces, pizzas, casseroles, etc.). Hard grating cheese (Parmesan, Romano as well as semi soft varieties like Swiss, Cheddar, and Mozzarella) can be more successfully frozen than soft cheeses (Brie, Camembert).

Slicing apples

Apples tend to brown very quickly after being diced or sliced. Add 10ml (2 teaspoons) of lemon juice to a bowl of water and place the cut apples in the lemon water until served or added to a recipe. The apples will keep their colour and texture perfectly.

Frying technique

A simple technique can help prevent breaded or battered foods from sticking when preparing them in a basket-type fryer. When the oil has reached the desired temperature, hold the food item with tongs away from the sides and bottom of the pan and partially submerge it in the oil for 10 seconds before releasing it to cook. This sets the coating and makes it less likely to adhere to the fryer's basket.

Over-spiced dish?

If you've overdone the spices in a dish, a bit of sugar will balance it out. Lemon juice also helps so put in half a lemon, cook for a few minutes then remove.

Quick tip

BURNT RICE

If you burn a pot of rice, place a slice of white bread on the top of the rice. Let it sit for a few minutes. The burnt taste will absorbed into the bread and the rice will taste fine.
Be sure not to scrape the bottom of the pan when serving.

Smooth running salt cellar

To avoid your salt cellar clogging up, put a few grains of rice in with the salt, this will absorb the moisture which causes the salt to stick together and the cellar to clog.

Bread revival

To revive a stale French loaf, cut it into thick slices almost to the base then spread garlic butter between the slices. Wrap in foil, and bake in a hot oven for ten minutes. A slightly stale loaf of bread can be perked up by placing it in a colander over a saucepan of boiling water. Cover with the pan lid until the bread is warm.

Wait before salting meat

Never salt meat before cooking as it will draw out all the juices and toughen the meat.

Does that knife need sharpening?

Every kitchen should have a good sharpening steel as part of the knife set. The main misconception, however, is that a steel actually sharpens the knife – it doesn't! The purpose of the steel is to finely tune the edge of a knife by removing the metal burrs caused by normal use. This is done every time the knife appears 'dull'. When the knife needs to be sharpened again, this must be done using a proper sharpening stone and oil or carried out professionally. Good quality knives will last much longer if they are looked after in this way.

Non-stick cheese

To keep cheese from sticking to the grater first spray the grater with non-stick cooking spray – it works a treat!

Easy-peel hard-boiled eggs

A few simple tips can make peeling hard-boiled eggs easy. Add the fresh eggs to a saucepan of cold water containing 1 teaspoon of salt. Bring to a boil, cover and remove from the heat. Allow the eggs to sit in the water for about 15 minutes. Drain off the warm water and place the eggs in iced water. Allow to chill thoroughly before peeling.

Salted or unsalted butter?

Are there any advantages to using unsalted butter? Some cooks believe it is better to add salt to a dish as needed rather than to be locked in on the salt content of an ingredient. Salt can also mask the off flavour of butter that isn't at its freshest point. Because dessert recipes use very little salt, using unsalted butter can definitely help assure the desired end result.

Fresher packed lunches

To keep packed lunches fresh and at a safe temperature, freeze a part of the lunch, e.g. a small tub of yoghurt or a carton of fruit juice. Pop this into an insulated lunch bag and it will keep the rest of the food nicely chilled until lunchtime.

Freezing stock

If you have any flavoursome, unused stock left over after cooking then don't waste it. It can be stored easily by freezing in ice cube trays and keeping in a plastic bag in the freezer.

STORING EGGS

It is best to store eggs in the refrigerator as this slows down the aging and therefore they will keep longer. Store them in a carton to prevent them from losing moisture and being tainted by nearby strong flavoured food. Always store eggs with the pointed end down as this keeps the yolk in the centre and helps to keep the egg fresh.

Perfect melted chocolate

Following a few simple guidelines can help ensure success when melting chocolate for a recipe. First make sure that the bowl (stainless steel or glass) is totally dry and add the chocolate to the bowl in small pieces. Always place the bowl over steaming, not boiling water.

A microwave oven also works well for melting chocolate. Place the chocolate pieces in a microwaveable dish. Set the oven on medium power (50%) and heat for 40 seconds for 28g (1oz), 1 minute for 57g (2oz), 2 minutes for 113g (4oz) and 3 minutes for 226g (8oz). Stop the oven and stir once halfway through the melting process.

Buying cauliflowers

When buying cauliflowers always pull back the leaves to make sure the florets are white all the way around the head.

Keep a check on herbs and spices

It is reasonably obvious to say that dried herbs and spices will not last forever! For the best flavour they should be used within two years of packaging. Usage after this time is safe, but some loss of flavour might be noticeable. Proper storage of spices will ensure maximum flavour and colour retention. Heat, light and moisture are all enemies of dried spices. Heat causes flavour loss, light will fade the naturally bright colours, and moisture can cake ground and powdered spices. Keep spices in a cool, dry, and dark cupboard away from the cooker or intense heat.

It is best to open and visually check spices and herbs annually. Crush a small amount of the spice or herb in your hand and smell it. If the aroma is not rich, full and immediate, the spice or herb has probably lost much of its potency. The exceptions are whole spices such as peppercorns and cinnamon sticks. These have a protective outer coating and will not release their full fragrance until broken or crushed.

Compare the aroma of a freshly purchased spice or herb to that which you've stored for a year or more to see the difference. Be aware, however, that subtle changes might also occur with each new crop of herb or spice. Green, leafy herbs will fade upon ageing but different herbs naturally vary in colour and should not always be compared with each other. Tarragon, for example, is naturally greener in colour than rosemary. Also some dill products contain the flower portion, giving them a more yellow colour than those without the inclusion of flowers. Red coloured spices, such as paprika, red pepper and chilli powder, will turn from red to brown in colour with age, however they might still be perfectly okay to use.

Spices and herbs are made up of numerous flavour components. Each component dissipates at varying rates, altering the overall balance of flavours as they age. The initial quality of a spice and herb can have an impact on its shelf life, with a high quality product retaining its good flavour longer than a lower quality version.

SOURED CREAM

To make soured cream simply add one teaspoon of lemon juice to 150ml (¼ pint) of single cream. Stir well and leave to thicken.

Cooking spinach

To cook spinach quickly and retain its quality, buy washed spinach in the sealed plastic bags from the supermarket, make a couple of holes in the top and cook in a microwave on high for 90 seconds. Open the bag and serve immediately. Quick cooking like this means that the days of soggy spinach have gone!

Preserving with lemon juice

Most cooks know that to keep an avocado looking good you squeeze lemon or lime juice over it as soon as you expose its flesh to air. However lemon juice also prevents peaches, bananas, apples, and pears from turning brown, as well as bringing out their best flavours.

Oven temperature

Check the accuracy of your oven temperature by placing an oven thermometer in the centre of the oven. Heat to 200°C/400°F/gas 6 and compare. If there is a large discrepancy then in future adjust the cooking temperature accordingly or, better still, call in an engineer to replace the thermostat.

HEATING CREAM

If you want to heat cream for a recipe then use double cream that does not separate as easily as single or soured cream. Alternatively you can substitute crème fraiche.

Cutting in

You might come across the term 'cut in' when preparing certain baking recipes. This means to combine a dry ingredient (like flour) with a solid fat (usually butter or margarine). The end result should be small, crumb-like particles. This can be done easily by using the pulse feature of a food processor. Other methods include working the ingredients between two knives or gently kneading them with your fingers.

Keeping butter

Unsalted butter will keep in a freezer for six months, but salted butter will successfully freeze for only three months.

Extra virgin olive oil

Olive oils labelled 'extra virgin' must have an acidity level below 1%. They usually come from the first pressing of the olives. A good extra virgin olive oil should be used as a condiment and never used for cooking. The fruity flavour is somewhat subtle. Sprinkle it over bread, fresh Mozzarella or salad greens.

The perfect cup of coffee

If you make your coffee with tap water, let the water run for a while to add extra oxygen. This will give your coffee a much fuller-bodied flavour. To make the perfect cup of coffee, like the ones you buy in the best coffee bars, always use 2 tablespoons of ground coffee per 175ml (6 fl.oz) of water.

Roasting on a rack

Roasting meats on a rack can be beneficial in two ways. First it allows excess fat to drip off and not be included in the final dish. It also lets the heat circulate completely around the meat, which makes for even cooking. It is especially useful for items like poultry or a leg of lamb.

Feta cheese

Cubes of feta cheese can be stored in a jar of olive oil with sprigs of herbs or garlic cloves added for flavour, if desired. The wonderfully flavoured oil can be used later for salad dressings.

Cooking fish

Selecting the best way to prepare particular varieties of fish can help ensure the success of a meal. Basically, most fish fall into two categories: fatty and lean. Fatty fish include trout, tuna, salmon, and swordfish. These types benefit from 'dry' cooking methods like grilling, baking, or broiling. The lean fish include cod, sole, and bass. They are best cooked using a 'wet' method like steaming, frying, or poaching. Ask your fishmonger about the fat content of a particular variety.

Snacks in a hurry

Making quick snacks or light meals is easy if you keep a few items in the cupboard. The formula is bread item + cheese + sauce + meat (optional). An example would be tortillas + cheddar + salsa + beef = burrito. Remember that the bread items usually freeze well.

Try combinations of the following to create new dishes ...

- Muffins.
- Pitta.
- Cheeses (like Cheddar and Mozzarella).
- Salsa.
- Minced beef (browned and frozen).
- Italian pasta sauce (jar).
- Cooked frozen diced chicken.
- Tortillas.
- Tinned meat (ham, corned beef etc.).
- Onions.

ICE CUBES

To store ice cubes for a party remove from the ice trays and place on a baking sheet in the freezer for a couple of hours. You can then store them in a bag without them sticking together.

What does scoring mean?

Whilst I am sure that all your meals will get 10 out of 10, the technique of scoring involves making shallow cuts into foods before cooking! This is done for several reasons. It can allow a marinade to enter and therefore flavour meats more easily, help cuts of beef flatten out and thus cook evenly, or it is sometimes used to tenderise foods. The thickest parts of a fish are often scored to assure even cooking. Ham is often cut in this way to create a decorative design.

Pasta or noodles?

The main difference between pastas and noodles is that most noodles contain egg (or egg yolks) and most pasta does not. There are exceptions to this rule. Some recipes for making fresh pasta call for egg to be added. There are also 'no-yolk' noodles available! People on restricted diets may wish to check the listed ingredients before choosing which product to purchase.

Instant thickening

Instant potato powder or granules are excellent for thickening gravy, soups etc. as they won't make lumps like flour often does.

White or brown rice?

There are a few facts you might wish to consider when choosing rice for a recipe. Brown rice (whole grain with only the husk removed) is higher in fibre and more nutritious. It has a nutty flavour and chewy texture that may not be suitable for some preparations. Brown rice also takes longer to cook. Processed white rice has a neutral flavour and tends to take on the flavours of the ingredients it is prepared with. Choose the right rice product for the desired end result.

Freezing cream

Open freeze double cream in an ice cube tray, then turn out the cubes into polythene bags for storing in the freezer. The frozen cream cubes can be added straight into hot soups, sauces or casseroles.

Overcooked vegetables

If you overcook carrots, peas, parsnips or swede then drain well, place in a food processor and puree until smooth. Add a little cream to taste and, hey presto, you have a rich creamy vegetable puree!

Weekly refrigerator check

It's a good idea to make a weekly 'quality check' of the contents of your refrigerator. This can save you a lot of money. Always check the freshness of your vegetables. If they are starting to fade it might be a good time to make soup! Leftover meats should also be examined and disposed of if they are over their recommended fridge storage times.

Wooden skewers

Grilling foods on skewers makes for great presentation. Following a few guidelines can help ensure success. Be sure to soak wooden skewers in water for about 20 minutes before pushing on the food, and wrap the exposed 'handle' end with aluminium foil. Both of these techniques will help prevent the wood burning. To prevent over- or under-cooking of individual items, partially cook long-cooking foods (like peppers and onions) before placing them on skewers with fast-cooking items such as chicken, mushrooms and cherry tomatoes.

Quick tip

DRIED MUSHROOMS
To revive mushrooms that have dried out, add a little red wine and leave to soak for a few minutes. Then bring to the boil, stir in a little cream and chopped parsley and serve.

Keeping bread fresh

If you don't have a bread bin or crock, keep bread fresh by using a clean, dry tea towel or a cotton drawstring bag. Wash and dry the bag regularly to prevent mould from developing. A loaf can also be kept on a wooden breadboard and covered with an upturned earthenware bowl.

Marinating

Marinades for barbecues can be created easily by remembering that they are made by using three basic food types:

Oil: Any type from corn oil to olive oil.

Acid: This could be wine, fruit juice, or vinegar.

Seasonings: Herbs and spices to suit the food you are preparing.

Experiment with different combinations to create your own scrumptious summer recipes.

Freezing dough

If you make your own bread, any leftover, un-risen dough can be wrapped up well and frozen for about a month.

Freezing a gateau

When freezing a large cake or gateau, cut it into slices before freezing, and interleave each slice with a piece of non-stick greaseproof paper. Reassemble the cake and freeze as usual. You can then remove as many slices as you need without having to thaw the whole cake.

Safe knife storage

A safe way to store sharp kitchen knives is in a slot cut into the back of a worktop behind a drawer unit. The blades are then hidden behind the drawer and out of the way of small children.

Quick tip

SAVING ENERGY

If you have solid electric rings, then save energy by turning them off a few minutes before you finish cooking. The food will continue to cook on the remaining heat.

Freshly ground pepper

Many cooks would consider a pepper mill more of a necessity than a gadget. The taste of freshly-ground pepper over pre-ground can be compared with the difference between fresh herbs and the dried varieties. Keep one mill in the kitchen for cooking and one on the table for seasoning.

Fresh corn

Fresh corn kernels (as opposed to canned or frozen) can add flavour to most recipes. Corn can easily be removed form the cob by following a few simple tips. After removing the husk and silk, stand the ear on its end on a cutting board. Hold the corn using a clean dishtowel and carefully run a sharp knife down the ear, pressing the knife against the cob at a slight angle to remove the kernels.

Burnt hob

Try this to remove food burnt around a solid hob: once the hob has cooled, place a kitchen cloth in a solution of washing up liquid and water, wring it out and place onto the hob. Leave for two hours and then wipe clean.

Quick tip

EASY SLICING OF DRIED FRUIT
In recipes calling for dates, apricots or prunes, you will find the dried fruit easier to work with, especially to slice, if you chill it first in the refrigerator or even the freezer. The colder the fruit is, the easier it is to chop or slice.

Adding fruit to batter

If you're adding dried fruit to a cake or bread batter, coat the pieces of fruit with flour before adding to the mix. This will keep the fruit from dropping through the batter and appearing at the bottom of the cake or loaf.

Storing vegetable oils

All vegetable oils should be stored in a cool, dark cabinet to protect them from light, heat, and air. When exposed to air, fatty acids become rancid, which means they combine with oxygen to form hydro peroxides, natural substances that taste bad, smell bad, and even destroy the oh-so-good-for-you vitamin E in the oil.

Cleaning chrome trim

To clean rust from chrome trim in the kitchen, rub it with a piece of aluminium foil, 'shiny' side out, then buff with a soft cloth.

Simple classy garnish

You can create a simple and colourful garnish for most dishes using bell peppers. Purchase one each of the green, red and yellow varieties. Split them lengthwise. Remove the seeds and membranes and cut them into 50mm (2") strips. Place the "shiny" side down on a cutting board. Carefully slice off the inner part (using a horizontal motion) leaving only brightly coloured outer skin. Dice into tiny 2mm ($\frac{1}{16}$ inch) squares. Sprinkle on foods or on the rim of the plate.

Microwaving wedges

When cooking wedge-shaped items in a microwave, point the narrow side towards the middle of the microwave and the item will cook more evenly.

Protect non-stick pans

To protect the non-stick linings of pans when stacked together, place a sheet of kitchen paper between each pan before storing.

Chilled wrap

Keep a roll of plastic wrap or cling film in the fridge as this makes it easy to find the end and unwrap.

Safe cutting

Prevent injuries while slicing and dicing by following a few simple tips ...

- Always place a damp towel under the cutting board to limit movement.

- Be sure to get a 'flat side down' before preparing round items like onions or lemons. This can be done by cutting them down the middle and placing the flat side on the board before chopping.

- Always wash, bleach and rinse the board after each use, especially when cutting meat, poultry or seafood. If possible, have separate boards for fresh meats, cooked meats and vegetables.

Blanching

Recipes sometimes call for a technique called blanching or parboiling. This is the process whereby the item is quickly cooked (usually in boiling water) for a brief period of time. The food is usually refreshed afterwards in cold water to stop the cooking. This method is often used in preparing fresh vegetables for freezing.

Cleaning aluminium

To remove stains from an aluminium pan, fill it with water, add the juice of a lemon, and simmer gently until the metal brightens up.

Freezing minced meat

The freezing of minced beef (or any minced meat) can be made easier by following a few simple tips. First purchase good quality large plastic freezer bags. Place only 450 grams of minced meat in each bag and flatten the meat to a thin layer. Press to remove as much air as possible then seal the bag and freeze. This method allows for quick, safe freezing and for the meat to be thoroughly defrosted in the microwave oven without the usual browning around the edges.

12 'musts' for the kitchen cupboard

A well-stocked cupboard is the key to creating good meals in a hurry. Among the items you need to keep in the house are ...

Stock (beef and chicken)	Cornflour
Milk powder	Rice
Dijon mustard	Sugar
Olive oil	Flour
Canned diced tomatoes	Pasta
Good quality spaghetti sauce	Onions

To this basic list add your own items to accommodate your family's individual tastes.

Cleaning enamel

To clean badly stained enamel pans, fill with a solution of two teaspoons bleach to a pint of water. Leave to soak for one hour and then rinse thoroughly.

Cleaning copper

To clean copper pans, make a thick paste of flour and vinegar.
Use a kitchen cloth to rub over the copper until it is clean.
Finally wash in hot water and dry.

Reheating food

Cooked food, whether prepared at home or purchased, should
not be reheated more than once. When food is reheated it
should be heated until it is piping hot. Cooked food should
not be kept warm, it should be kept piping hot or it should be
cooled quickly and correctly stored – or eaten!

OPENED CANS
Empty the contents of a part used tin of food into a bowl,
cover and refrigerate. Never store food in part emptied
cans as the inside of the tin will begin to discolour and
taint the food.

Safe storage

Always store raw meats and food to be defrosted beneath
any cooked foods to avoid contamination from dripping juices.
Leave foods wrapped unless their packaging recommends you
do otherwise.

Salt substitution

To add to the flavour of most vegetables add a little fresh lemon juice instead of salt; this is most helpful to people on low salt diets.

Chilling bulk cooking

Foods that are prepared in large batches (soups and stews) are especially susceptible to harmful spoilage. It is always advisable to cool down the foods before placing them in the refrigerator. One way to do this is to add ice to your sink (with the plug in place). Place the pot of food on the ice and add water to the sink (about ¾ of the way up the side of the pan). Stir the food frequently. When chilled cover and refrigerate. Another quick way to chill is to transfer the soup or stew to a shallow baking pan (like a lasagne dish) before refrigerating. This allows a faster, safer cool down.

Smelly flask?

To keep a vacuum flask fresh, add a teaspoon of white sugar to the clean dry empty flask before storing it. This will prevent stale smells from developing inside the closed flask.

Steaming asparagus

If you don't want to buy a special asparagus steamer, then use a deep saucepan and make a ring of baking foil to hold the asparagus heads out of the water so that they only steam while the bottoms boil in the water.

Skimming soups

When making soups it is a good idea to skim the fat and 'foam' (impurities that rise to the top) during the early stages of cooking. Add any dried herbs after this process has been completed, as the herbs have a light texture and tend to also rise at this point, so if you've already added them they would be removed with the fat and impurities!

Quick tomato and red pepper soup

1 can chopped tomatoes

1 red pepper – deseeded and roughly chopped

500ml (1pt) chicken or vegetable stock

A dash of cream for decoration (optional)

Put tomatoes into a saucepan and add the red pepper. Then add the stock, bring to the boil and simmer for five minutes. Finally liquidise until smooth and serve with a swirl of cream if you want to be naughty!

What are crudités?

Easy additions to your party buffet are crudités – a selection of raw vegetables. Cut celery, carrots, broccoli, cauliflower or any other vegetable you enjoy into easy to pick up and dip pieces. Arrange them decoratively on a platter with your favourite dip or salad dressing. This offers your guests a lighter choice than some of the higher calorie items you might be offering later.

Dry marinating

'Dry rubs' are blends of ingredients (usually herbs, spices and salt) that are used to season meats just before grilling or smoking. For a fuller flavour allow the seasoned meats to marinate overnight in the refrigerator. Ensure that the product is covered with plastic wrap.

Saving scraps for stock

Stocks are the heart of great soups and sauces. Lots of items can be saved for stock making. Bag up carrot peels, onion skins, celery ends, parsley stems, and mushroom stems for use in preparing stocks. Other ingredients, from fish bones to chicken carcasses, can be frozen and contribute to a later stock.

Quick tip

SHARPENING SERRATED KNIVES
You should never sharpen serrated knives with a normal sharpening steel. When they are losing their 'edge' take them to a professional sharpener, unless you have a special sharpener for serrated knives.

Steaming without a steamer

To steam vegetables when you have not got a steamer use a metal sieve and a wide saucepan. Make sure that the sieve sits above the boiling water. Put the vegetables in the sieve and cover with a lid.

GREEN POTATOES

Don't be overly concerned if your potato has a greenish tinge on the skin. It is simply a chemical reaction caused by exposure to light. It can, however, cause a bitter taste so peel the potato before using. To prevent this occurring, store potatoes away from any light source.

Tricky pouring!

Try lightly spraying your measuring jug with oil before adding thick ingredients like treacle or honey. This will help insure that the entire contents (and the correct measurement) go into your recipe. It also makes cleanup easier and reduces waste.

Freezing herbs

Freezing rather than drying better preserves some herbs. You will sacrifice the fresh texture, but retain more of the flavour by freezing basil, chives, dill, parsley, and tarragon. Try to use frozen herbs within six months of harvesting.

Perfect thickening

When thickening with cornflour and water, always bring the food being cooked to a gentle boil before reducing the heat to a simmer. This will ensure that the thickener will reach its full degree of effectiveness.

What does 'butterfly' mean?

Sometimes you'll see the term 'butterfly' in a recipe. This means that the food item is split down the middle, without cutting it into two pieces. The end result is thought to resemble a butterfly. 'Butterflying' makes foods easier to stuff and can reduce cooking times.

Fragrant sugars

To make vanilla sugar, bury two vanilla pods in a jar of sugar and leave for at least a week, shaking the jar occasionally. In addition to vanilla pods, wonderfully flavoured sugars can be produced by storing with lemon zest, rose petals, or lavender.

Quick tip

NO SOUR CREAM?
To make soured cream: add 5ml (one teaspoon) of lemon juice to 150ml (¼ pint) of single cream, stir well and then leave to thicken for 30 minutes.

Experiment with pesto

The ingredients in classic pesto (usually basil, olive oil, garlic, pine nuts and Parmesan) can be changed to create exciting new sauces. Different fresh herbs (or combinations) can be substituted. When using strong herbs (like tarragon or dill), try mixing them with equal parts of parsley. Walnuts are great in pesto. For a different flavour, try lightly toasting any nut used.

Breading foods

Use this procedure to add flavour and to protect foods when frying or sautéing ...

Flour: Dredge the item to be cooked in plain or seasoned flour. This will help the breading adhere to the food.

Egg wash: A basic mixture is 2 beaten eggs plus ½ cup milk. Dip the floured item in the wash. Drain off any excess before going to the next step. This will help bind the breading and add moisture.

Crumbs: Breadcrumbs (fine or fresh) are commonly used. Other items are sometimes used. Cover the food well with the crumbs and gently press them in before cooking.

No corkscrew?

To uncork a bottle of wine without a corkscrew, screw a metal hook into the cork, put a wooden spoon handle through the hook, and pull the cork out. Cheers!

Accurate measuring

Proper measuring is essential when preparing food from a written recipe. Always assume that amounts are in 'level' teaspoons or tablespoons unless otherwise stated.

Pureeing acid fruits

To purée acid fruits, such as raspberries, use a nylon sieve and a wooden spoon, as metal sieves and spoons may react with the acid in the fruit, and discolour the puree.

Buying stewing beef

Avoid the pre-cut diced 'stewing beef' in your supermarket's meat department. The pieces are usually end trimmings from various cuts and the price is often inflated. Your best bet is to buy a whole piece of beef and simply dice it yourself.

Special diets

Most recipes can be modified to accommodate special dietary needs. First isolate the ingredients that are undesirable. For example, someone on a low-fat diet would look for items like butter, eggs, milk, or cheese. These foods can be substituted with vegetable oil, eggbeaters, skimmed milk, and fat-free cheese. Remove chicken skin to reduce fat. Experiment with changing a high-fat cooking process (like frying) to sautéing or grilling.

Food storage

Avoid keeping ingredients like herbs, oils, pastas and vinegars too near to the oven. The extreme heat can seriously alter the flavour of these delicate items. Also, never keep glass containers of any kind close to the heat of the cooker.

Buying fresh spinach

When purchasing fresh spinach look for dark green leaves with firm texture. Always wash spinach (even the pre-washed product). To store, dry the leaves using a spinner if possible, wrap in paper towels, place in a plastic food bag and refrigerate.

No shallots?

Shallots are an ingredient that many cooks don't always keep on hand. Using onions and garlic can make an acceptable substitute. For every tablespoon of shallots needed substitute a mix of $2/3$ tablespoon of minced onion to $1/3$ tablespoon of minced garlic.

Quick tip

CRYSTALLIZED HONEY

If your runny honey isn't runny anymore but has begun to crystallize, stand the jar in a bowl of hot water for five minutes turning the jar a few times until the honey becomes clear and liquid.

Celery revival

To revive sticks of limp celery, place them in a bowl of ice-cold water for an hour. Adding a squeeze of fresh lemon to the water will greatly improve the flavour too.

Avoiding kitchen knife cuts

- Don't store knives in a drawer. It's easy to forget they are there when you are in a hurry.

- Never put sharp knives in a sink full of water.

- Never attempt to catch a falling knife. Let it fall.

- Always use a cutting board. Never slice food while holding it in your hand.

Storing pesto

When storing pesto in your refrigerator, cover the surface with a thin layer of olive oil and seal the container tightly. This will keep the flavour fresh for several days and prevent the product from darkening.

Chiffonade

If you come across the fancy term 'chiffonade' in a recipe it simply means the method of cutting vegetables or herbs into thin strips.

Pan sizes

This might sound obvious but always use tins and saucepans of the right size when cooking! When roasting make sure the roasting tin is large enough to hold the food and any juices it may produce, thus preventing fat from spitting over the sides or hot juices being spilt when moving the tin. When cooking liquids make sure the saucepan, casserole dish, or other container is large enough so that boiling liquids do not splash or bubble over, and again so it can be moved easily without spilling the hot liquid.

Whipping cream

To create whipped cream with perfect texture, make sure the mixer bowl, beaters, and cream are well chilled. This also speeds up the time it takes to reach the 'firm peaks' stage. Be careful not to over-whip.

Separating eggs

To successfully separate an egg yolk from its white, carefully break the egg in half and tip the yolk carefully from one half shell to the other a number of times, letting the egg white fall into a bowl underneath as you do it. Alternatively, gently break the egg onto a saucer, place an egg-cup carefully over the yolk and whilst holding this firmly in place tip the egg white into a bowl, leaving the egg yolk under the egg cup. If a little egg yolk falls into the white whilst separating, use the eggshell as a scoop to collect it. The egg yolk is collected easily in this way, unlike trying to capture it with a spoon.

Storing tomatoes

Only store tomatoes in a fridge if they are ripe. You should not put under ripe tomatoes in the fridge as low temperatures spoil the ripening process.

Quick tip

REVIVING COOKED CARROTS
To add to the flavour of previously cooked carrots sprinkle a little orange juice over them just before reheating.

Just enough marinade!

Some marinades are expensive to make. In order to prepare the correct amount, a simple formula can be handy. In general, make ¼ of a cup of marinade for every 450g (1lb) of meat. Frequent turning of the food can also stretch the marinade.

Cleaning processors and blenders

Some foods can get stuck in groves and seams when using a food processor or blender. These are possible places for harmful bacteria to grow. Cleaning the sharp blades is always a potential safety hazard. A quick way to clean these appliances is to let them clean themselves. Add warm water about $\frac{1}{3}$ of the way up and add a dash of dishwashing liquid or $\frac{1}{4}$ dishwashing tablet. Run the appliance until it is clean, rinse with warm water and allow to air dry.

Frozen lemon

Slice fresh lemons, open freeze on a tray, then pack in the usual manner. Always there for that gin and tonic! Also try a slice of cucumber in gin and tonic instead of lemon. So refreshing!

Lighter batter

You can achieve a lighter batter when preparing foods by using liquids with carbonation instead of the water or milk stated in many recipes. Beer is great for full-flavoured foods because it also adds a little flavour of its own. Use it in batters for fish and onion rings. Foods like vegetable fritters are best when soda water replaces some of liquids in the batter.

Odour-free chopping board

After using a chopping board to prepare strong smelling foods, wash the board and then wipe over with a cut lemon. This will eliminate any odours.

Storing mushrooms

Store mushrooms in a paper bag at the bottom of the fridge.

Banish bacteria

Keep surfaces and equipment as clean as possible during the preparation of foods. Bacteria multiply rapidly in damp warm conditions, so a damp surface in the warmth of a kitchen is an ideal environment for them. There is also the benefit that the more cleaning that is done during the preparation process the less there is to be done at the end. Always wash and dry your hands thoroughly, with soap and hot water, before and after preparing food. This will help prevent the cross contamination of bacteria to the food that is being prepared.

Storing citrus

To store citrus fruits for longer than a week, wipe each fruit and wrap in newspaper. Pack into a polystyrene bag or box and store in a cool dry place.

No self-raising flour?

If you are short of self-raising flour use plain flour with the addition of baking powder. The amount to add varies depending upon what is being cooked; however a usual amount would be 1 level teaspoon of baking powder to 113g (4oz) of flour.

Storing celery

Celery will keep for weeks in a fridge when wrapped in kitchen foil.

Lemon juice cubes

Like most fruit juices, lemon juice does not keep for very long before it loses its fresh taste in cooking. Fortunately, lemon juice can easily be frozen in ice cube trays so that it is always available when required. When a recipe calls for a tablespoon of lemon juice – just toss in a cube!

Quick tip

ODOUR-FREE HANDS

If you have been preparing fish, onion or garlic dishes and your hands smell to high Heaven, simply rub your hands over a stainless steel bowl, pan or other kitchen gadget – even the stainless steel taps – and the smell should disappear.

Alternatively try washing your hands with lemon juice or dampening them and rubbing with salt before rinsing under running water.

Safe slicing

When slicing vegetables, use your knuckle to guide the knife and fold the finger tips back to prevent accidents.

Keep vegetables green

When boiling green vegetables, keep the lid off the saucepan and they will stay greener!

Useful substitutes

Breadcrumbs	Crushed cream crackers or cornflakes
Cornflour (1 tablespoon as a thickener)	2 level tablespoons plain flour
Single Cream – 285ml (½ pint)	225ml (8fl.oz) milk plus 60ml (2fl.oz) melted unsalted butter
Honey – 225ml (8fl.oz)	225g (8oz) sugar plus 4 tablespoons water or golden syrup
Lemon juice (1 teaspoon)	½ teaspoon vinegar or lime juice
Ice Cream	Frozen yoghurt
Whole milk – 285ml (½ pint)	285ml (½ pint) skimmed milk plus 3 teaspoons melted butter
Noodles	Spaghetti
Tartare sauce	7 tablespoons mayonnaise plus 2 tablespoons chopped sweet mixed pickles
Tomato Sauce	Condensed tomato soup or a packet of tomato soup made up with half quantity of water
Gravy	Condensed tinned soup or packet soup made up with half the usual quantity of water

Bitter almonds

The dark skin on whole almonds can sometimes add a bitter flavour. They might also make an undesirable visual presentation in some recipes. Simply add the almonds to a saucepan and cover with water. Bring to a boil, drain, and shock with cold water. Squeeze the almonds and most skins will come right off. Place the nuts on a baking sheet at 150°C/300°F/gas 2 for five minutes to crisp them back up.

Joint temperature

Make sure large joints of meat or poultry are cooked right through to the centre. A meat thermometer or probe is relatively inexpensive and can be used to check the final temperature in the centre of the item being cooked. Most harmful bacteria are killed when the temperature in the centre of the food reaches 70°C (160°F) for two or more minutes. As anyone who has ever experienced food poisoning will tell you – this is so worth doing!

Quick tip

FRESH HERBS

Fresh herbs can add new levels of flavour to most recipes. Use two teaspoons of fresh, chopped herbs in place of one teaspoon of the dried equivalent. The flavour and intensity of most herb varieties are concentrated in the dehydration process.

Cooking perfect pasta

When cooking pasta it is not necessary to add oil to the water. The oil stays mainly on the surface and adds little to the taste. Cook the pasta in a pan of boiling, salted water. When cooked, drain and then pour extra virgin or virgin oil over and shake well. This will prevent the pasta from sticking together, and also give you all the flavour of the oil.

Greasy wrappers

Use the outer wrappers from packets of butter, lard etc. to grease and/or line baking tins.

Quick tip

ONIONS WITHOUT TEARS

To stop your eyes shedding tears when chopping an onion make sure that the knife is razor sharp. If the knife is blunt it squeezes the moisture out when it gets to the cell walls, instead of cutting straight through them. The resulting liquid is what makes the tear ducts run.

Frozen herbs

If you have a glut of fresh herbs here's a great way to store them ... Take an ice cube tray, finely chop the fresh herbs and place some into each section of the tray. Add a little fresh water to each section and then freeze. Remove the frozen cubes of herbs and add to recipes as required.

Soup for sauce

Use condensed soup as a quick and easy sauce. A great example is to cut some leftover chicken into cubes and mix with either condensed chicken or mushroom soup and serve on a bed of rice. "Chicken a la King" in minutes!

Freezing bread

When freezing sliced bread place greaseproof between the slices so that you can remove just the number of slices you need without having to thaw the whole loaf.

Pastry mix

Save precious time by mixing your pastry to the 'breadcrumb' stage (i.e. rubbing in the flour and fat), and then put this mixture into an airtight container in the freezer. It is a good idea to make quite a large amount. When you want to make pastry, take out enough of the dry mixture for your requirements and add the water in the usual way (1 teaspoon of water for every 25g (1oz) of mixture). This mixture can also be used to make crumble by just adding sugar.

Quick jackets

For a better textured baked potato than those that you microwave try this method for speeding up the potato baking process. Pre-heat the oven to 200°C/400°F/gas 6. Place the potato in boiling water for 10 minutes, and then bake for 30 minutes. This will cut the cooking time in half.

Blow-dried jar

To dry a tall spaghetti jar quickly after washing, use a hair dryer!

Freezer rules

- Do not refreeze food after it has been thawed.
- Thawed raw food can be frozen after it has been cooked.
- Thawed cooked food should not be refrozen.
- Check the contents of the freezer every so often to make sure that storage times for the particular foods are not exceeded.
- Always buy frozen foods as the last thing when shopping and take them straight to the freezer when you get home. Wrapping frozen items together, and placing them in an insulated bag or box, will help to prevent their temperature from rising.
- Food is best thawed placed in or on a suitable container in the fridge. Do not thaw items by placing them in hot or warm water as it will be difficult to determine if the centre has thawed properly, particularly with large joints of meat or poultry.

Piping hot is perfect!

Ovens and appliances can vary in their accuracy and efficiency, so always check that food is piping hot right through to the centre before serving. Even if you are following a recipe or instructions on the packaging of frozen foods, check to make sure that it is thoroughly cooked.

STORING FOODS

Cooked and fresh foods should not be stored in the same container. They should be packaged and stored separately. This will avoid cross contamination between stored items. Do not put warm food in the fridge, make sure it has been cooled correctly and quickly. This will avoid unnecessary changes in temperature and the formation of condensation, which can easily affect other items being stored as well as the efficiency of the fridge.

Meringue success

When making meringues use fresh egg whites. Old egg whites tend to collapse when other ingredients are folded in, and they don't rise well in the oven. Use eggs at room temperature as cold egg whites tend to reduce meringue volume. Don't make meringues on humid days as humidity causes meringues to be sticky and chewy.

Don't over beat egg whites, just beat them until foamy. A small amount of cream of tartar or vinegar can be added to the mixture at the beginning of whipping to help stabilize the foam and make it less likely to collapse. Never let any yolk get into the whites.

Bake meringues at low temperatures because they tend to brown quickly. Leave hard meringues in the oven after baking so they will cool slowly and not crack.

Christmas tips

Christmas is a most wonderful time of year. Family and friends meet to celebrate, and everything seems to buzz with excitement as festivities fill the air. The atmosphere should be one of happiness and giving. However, so often as Christmas approaches, panic surrounds us as we worry about how to entertain, what to serve, how much to cook, and so on. Here are a few tips to ease the anxiety ...

- The holiday spreads over several days and even into New Year, so careful planning is essential. If possible, plan for each day of this hectic period. Consider which foods will be left over (such as poultry and produce), and select recipes using these ingredients. Freeze food for unexpected arrivals.

- Make a fish and meat pâté, and freeze whole, or slice first (to thaw more quickly later). Served with a salad and crusty bread, a pâté makes a delicious, impromptu meal.

- Freeze a few puddings or gateaux for impressive desserts. Frozen finger foods also make marvellous standbys and certainly take the pressure out of entertaining at short notice, so prepare a selection to serve with drinks.

- Once you have planned menus and calculated how many visitors are expected, determine which recipes can be made in advance and frozen or stored until required, such as Christmas cakes, puddings, and mince pies. Make detailed lists of food to be purchased in advance and at the last minute. Several weeks beforehand, stock up on drinks and easily-stored ingredients for nibbles, avoiding the rush in the days leading up to Christmas.

- Edible gifts, such as preserves, brandied mincemeat, fruits in liqueurs, pretty sweets, and cookies are most attractive in baskets, boxes, or dainty glass or china dishes. Assorted cheeses make a nice last-minute present and look especially good in a basket with crackers, butter, and an attractive, festive napkin. Cookies or gingerbread houses serve as perfect novelty gifts for children. A mini-Christmas cake with a few mince pies is a most welcome offering for someone living alone, or make up a mini-hamper of homemade goodies, such as pâté, preserves, cake, Christmas pudding, and cookies.

So with good planning and thinking ahead we can take the stress out of Christmas! Now that you feel happier about the whole occasion, vow to get off to the best possible start by making lists of all the things you will need to do under different headings such as:

- Jobs to do e.g. tidy and clear fridge, freezer, cupboards, shelves etc.
- General food shopping e.g. flour, sugar etc.
- General non-food shopping e.g. turkey size foil, cling film etc.
- Week before Christmas e.g. eggs, bacon, frozen pastry.
- Last few days before Christmas e.g. potatoes, vegetables, fruit, bread etc.

Christmas day vegetables

Prepare vegetables like carrots, parsnips, Brussels sprouts etc. on Christmas Eve and store them in the refrigerator in sealed plastic bags.

To make serving easier, cook the vegetables a couple of hours earlier than you need them for the meal. When they are almost ready, drain them—keeping the water to make the gravy—then plunge the vegetables into cold water to stop the cooking process.

Place them into serving dishes, and microwave to reheat at the last moment.

Turkey

Now let's tackle the turkey! If you are going to buy a frozen turkey then buy it at the beginning of December when the shops are quiet. You need to allow 300g (12oz) of meat per person. When you get the turkey home, make a note somewhere in the kitchen of when you need to take the turkey out of the freezer. The importance of this cannot be over emphasised!

As well as the recommended thawing time you need to allow an extra 8–10 hours. The idea is to get the bird completely thawed out by Christmas Eve. You then need to place the turkey in a very cool room, such as a spare room with the radiator off, to bring it back to room temperature before cooking.

- For thawing in a fridge at 4°C, allow 12 hours per 1kg (2.2lb); so 4 days for a 8kg (17½lb) turkey.
- For thawing in a cool room at 15°C, allow 7 hours per 1kg (2.2lb); so 56 hours for a 8kg (17½lb) turkey.
- For thawing at room temperature at 20°C, allow 2 hours per 1kg (2.2lb); so 16 hours for an 8kg (17½lb) turkey.

Obviously your fridge or room may have a different temperature from those listed so you may need to allow more or less time than quoted.

A few tips for a perfect roast turkey!

- Cooking the stuffing in the turkey cavity is not recommended as it takes longer to cook the turkey, and it is also more difficult to make sure that the turkey is cooked through properly. It is acceptable (and very pleasant!) to use the cavity to tuck a bunch of herbs, a lemon, or a whole onion inside the carcass of a turkey before roasting. The flavour will penetrate the meat, and will make tasty juices for the gravy.

- Keep the breast of birds such as turkey, pheasant or pigeon moist and tender by laying bacon rind or streaky bacon over the breast before roasting.

- Cooking poultry in a roasting bag will eliminate the need for basting. If you want to crisp up the skin, open the bag for the final 20 minutes of cooking time.

- Before placing the turkey in a roasting tin, cover the base of the tin with celery sticks. These will act like a roasting rack and will add flavour to the meat juices to make a most delicious gravy.

- Instead of covering a large turkey with foil for roasting, dip a double layer of muslin into melted butter or oil, and lay it over the bird's skin. The muslin will allow the skin to brown and become crisp during cooking without trapping in steam as a covering of foil would do.

- Allow poultry to rest for about 20 minutes after roasting. This will make it easy to carve. Turn off the oven and leave the bird inside or remove and cover with foil.

And finally…

Even when most of the meat has been removed from your turkey, don't throw away the bones. Break up the carcass and place the pieces in a large pot. Cover with water. Add chopped onions, celery, carrots, and parsley to the pan. Simmer for a few hours and strain. Use this stock to make soups, gravy, and sauces. If, by now, you are a little tired of turkey, simply freeze it for later use when you want to re-live the flavours of Christmas!

And I find chopsticks frankly distressing. Am I alone in thinking it odd that a people ingenious enough to invent paper, gunpowder, kites and any number of other useful objects, and who have a noble history extending back 3,000 years haven't yet worked out that a pair of knitting needles is no way to capture food?

Bill Bryson

Conversion tables
& cooking times

section 2
Conversion tables & cooking times

To make this book as internationally accessible as possible I have included the following conversion charts so you can convert any recipe quantities you might encounter into imperial, metric or US measurements. Be sure to convert accurately as guess work can produce disastrous results for what might have been a great culinary success!

Weight conversions

To convert ...	Multiply by ...
Grams to ounces	0.0353
Grams to pounds	0.0022
Kilograms to pounds	2.2046
Kilograms to tons	0.00098
Tonnes to tons	0.9842
Ounces to grams	28.35
Pounds to grams	453.592
Pounds to kilograms	0.4536
Tons to kilograms	1016.05
Tons to tonnes	1.016

Quick weight conversions

2oz	57g
4oz	113g
8oz	227g
12oz	340g
1lb (16oz)	454g
1¼lb	567g
1½lb	680g
2lb	907g
30g	1oz
50g	1¾oz
100g	3½oz
125g	4½oz
150g	5Ðoz
200g	7oz
250g	9oz
500g	17½oz

Liquid conversions (approximate) – Imperial, Metric and US

Imperial	Metric	US Cups
½ fl.oz	15ml	1 level tablespoon
1 fl.oz	30ml	⅛ cup
2 fl.oz	60ml	¼ cup
3 fl.oz	90ml	⅜ cup
4 fl.oz	125ml	½ cup
5 fl.oz / ¼ pint	150ml	⅔ cup
6 fl.oz	175ml	¾ cup
8 fl.oz	250ml	1 cup
10 fl.oz/ ½ pint	300ml	1 ¼ cups
12 fl.oz	375ml	1 ½ cups
16 fl.oz	500ml	2 cups / 1 US pint
20 fl.oz / 1 pint	600ml	2 ½ cups
1 ½ pints	900ml	3 ¾ cups
1 ¾ pints	1 litre	4 cups / 1 quart
2 pints	1 ¼ litres	1 ¼ quarts
2 1/3 pints	1 ½ litres	3 US pints
3 ¼ pints	2 litres	2 quarts

Handy kitchen measures

The following are equivalent to approximately 28g (1oz) or:

1 level tablespoon	Salt
3 level tablespoons	Flour
2 level tablespoons	Rice
5 level tablespoons	Grated cheese
4 level tablespoons	Cocoa powder
1 level tablespoon	Honey/syrup/jam
2 level tablespoons	Granulated sugar
3 level tablespoons	Sifted icing sugar
6 level tablespoons	Fresh breadcrumbs
4 level tablespoons	Porridge oats

Oven temperatures

Fahrenheit (°F)	Celsius (°C)	Gas	Description
225	110	¼	Very slow
250	120/130	½	Very slow
275	140	1	Slow
300	150	2	Slow
325	160/170	3	Moderate
350	180	4	Moderate
375	190	5	Moderately hot
400	200	6	Moderately hot
425	220	7	Hot
450	230	8	Hot
475	240	9	Very hot

Spoon measures

1 tablespoon (tblsp)	3 teaspoons
1 level tablespoon (tblsp)	15 ml
1 level teaspoon (tsp)	5 ml

- A tablespoon or tblsp., when referring to dry goods (i.e. flour etc.), usually means a rounded tablespoon.

- A rounded tablespoon means there is as much of the product you are measuring above the top edge of the spoon as there is in the 'bowl' of the spoon.

- A heaped tablespoon means as much as you can get onto the spoon without it falling off.

- A level tablespoon is where the ingredient is level only with the top edge of the spoon. To achieve this, fill the spoon and then run a knife horizontally across the top, discarding anything above the level of the spoon. Of course, do make sure you have something underneath to catch it!

- A stick of butter is equal to half a cup (113g, 4 oz or 8 tablespoons).

Cooking times

Approximate cooking times are shown in the tables below. Different appliances might vary in their efficiency and cooking times are also affected by the position of shelves in the oven. Always make sure food is properly cooked before serving. A meat thermometer or probe can be used to check the final temperature in the centre of a joint or item being cooked.

If using a fan-assisted oven refer to the manufacturer's user manual for the necessary cooking adjustment. As a guide, lower the oven temperature by 20°C/40°F, or the cooking times by 15 per cent.

Roast chicken:

Cooked in the centre of the oven at 190C/375°F/gas 5, 20 mins per 450g (1lb) + 20 mins. When neck end is stuffed allow an extra five minutes per 450g (1lb).

- Test that it's cooked by pressing a skewer into the deepest part of each thigh; the juices released should be clear and not contain any blood.

- For carving, remove the chicken from the oven and allow it to rest for approximately five minutes. This allows the meat to set, making carving easier.

Roast meats:

Cooked in the centre of the oven at 180C/350°F/gas 4 to 190C/375°F/gas 5.

Meat	Rare	Medium	Well done
Beef	20 mins per 450g (1lb) + 20 mins	25 mins per 450g (1lb) + 25 mins	30 mins per 450g (1lb) + 30 mins
Lamb	–	25 mins per 450g (1lb) + 25 mins	30 mins per 450g (1lb) + 30 mins
Pork	–	30 mins per 450g (1lb) + 30 mins	35 mins per 450g (1lb) + 35 mins

- To check the meat is cooked, place on a tray and press firmly to make sure the juices released are clear and do not contain any blood.

- In general all meats should be cooked through.

- Pork must always be cooked thoroughly.

- Lamb may be served pink, but must be cooked through.

- Beef is normally served slightly underdone and a little blood should show in the juice.

- For carving, remove the joint from the oven and allow it to rest for approximately 10 minutes. This allows the meat to set, making carving easier, and reducing the tendency for the meat to shrink and curl.

Roast turkey:

Cooked in the centre of the oven at 190C/375°F/gas 5.

If wrapped in foil increase the overall cooking time by 15 minutes, removing the foil for the last 30 minutes to allow the skin to brown.

If you stuff the turkey add the weight of the stuffing to calculate the total weight.

Oven ready weight	Total cooking time
2.5–3kg (6–7lb)	2¼–2½ hours
3.5–4kg (8–9lb)	2½–3 hours
4.5–5kg (10–11lb)	3–3¼ hours
5.5–6kg (12–13lb)	3¼–3½ hours
6.5–7.5kg (14–17lb)	3½–3¾ hours
8–10kg (18–22lb)	3¾–4¼ hours
10.5kg plus (23lb plus)	4¼ hours plus

- Test that it's cooked by pressing a skewer into the deepest part of each thigh; the juices released should be clear and not contain any blood.

- For carving, remove the turkey from the oven and allow it to rest for approximately 10–15 minutes. This allows the meat to set, making carving easier.

Fish:

	Grill (mins)	Fry (mins)	Microwave (mins)	Steam (mins)	Bake (mins)	Poach (mins)
WHOLE FISH						
Plaice (300g)	13	5	3–4	20	18	5–6
Lemon sole (500g)	13	12	4–5	20	20	9
Dover sole (500g)	9	9	4–5	20	20	5
Dabs (400g)	9	9	3–4	20	20	4
Mackerel (300g)	15	15	3–4		25	
Sea bass (400g)	18	15	3–4	22	30	
Sea bream	18	15	3–4	22	30	
FILLETS (200G)						
Cod	17	5	3–4	15	18	5
Whiting	9	5	1–2	12	9	3–4
Lemon sole	9	4	1–2	12	9	3–4
Plaice	9	5	1–2	12	9	3–4
Turbot	9	6	2–3	12	12	5–8
STEAKS						
Cod	10	8–10	4–5	15	20	10

I don't like food that's too carefully arranged; it makes me think that the chef is spending too much time arranging and not enough time cooking. If I wanted a picture I'd buy a painting.

Andy Rooney

Peter's favourite recipes

Soups

Fat-free stock

This simple recipe makes about 1 litre of a flavourful, fat-free stock to add to soups and sauces.

2 medium onions
3 medium carrots
3 sticks celery
1 handful parsley with stems
3 cloves garlic, crushed
½ teaspoon thyme
2 bay leaves
1.5 litres (3pts) water
Salt and pepper to taste

- Place all the ingredients in a large soup pot. Bring to a boil, reduce the heat and simmer uncovered for 45 minutes.
- Strain and use immediately.
- Alternatively freeze or refrigerate until needed.

soups

Broccoli & Cheese Soup

Time to prepare: 5 minutes
Time to cook: 30 minutes

Serves 4

225g (8oz) broccoli
1 tablespoon sunflower oil
1 leek, thinly sliced
175g (6oz) potatoes, diced
Salt and Freshly ground black pepper
500ml (1pt) chicken stock (vegetable if vegetarian)
150ml (5fl.oz) dry white wine
113g (4oz) grated cheddar cheese

- Cut the stems from broccoli florets and cut into 13mm (½")
  pieces. Heat the oil in a pan.

- Add the leek, potatoes and broccoli and cook, stirring
  occasionally, for 5 minutes. Season with salt and pepper,
  and then add the stock and white wine and bring to a boil.
  Simmer 20 minutes, or until vegetables are tender.

- Puree in a blender or food processor and return to pan. Add
  cheese, reserving a little for garnish, and cook over low
  heat, stirring, until cheese is thoroughly melted into soup.

- Garnish with reserved cheese and serve.

*Note: Do not allow soup to boil after you add cheese or it will
become stringy.*

Roast Parsnip Soup

Time to prepare: 5 minutes   *Serves 4*
Time to cook: 60 minutes

450g (1lb) parsnips cut into chunks
1 tablespoon olive oil
Salt
Freshly ground black pepper
1 large potato, cut into chunks
1 large onion, chopped
850ml (1½pts) vegetable stock
2 tablespoons plain yogurt
1 large pinch of freshly grated nutmeg
Plain yogurt, to garnish
Freshly grated nutmeg, to garnish

- Lay the parsnips in bottom of a large pan and then drizzle with oil and season with salt and pepper.

- Cook over low heat 15–20 minutes, turning once, until browned all over. Add potato and onion and cook, stirring occasionally, 10 minutes. Add the stock, bring to the boil and simmer 35 minutes.

- Puree soup in a blender or food processor and return to pan. Stir in yogurt, nutmeg, salt and pepper and cook over low heat to warm through.

- Pour into warmed soup bowls, swirl in a little yogurt, sprinkle with nutmeg and serve.

soups

2am French Onion Soup

Time to prepare: 5 minutes   *Serves 4*
Time to cook: 30 minutes

I have called this '2am' because it was at this time of the morning, in a bistro in Montmatre, that I was shown how to make onion soup the French way.

60g (2oz) beef dripping
450g (1lb) large onions – sliced very thickly
30g (1oz) brown sugar
30g (1oz) plain flour
900 ml (30fl.oz) beef stock
Salt and freshly ground pepper

Optional:
French bread, Gruyere cheese, grated, Dijon mustard

- Peel and slice onions thickly and cook slowly in the butter until soft, but not brown. Then turn up the heat, add sugar and cook until the onions are just starting to caramelize.

- Stir in the flour, and cook for two minutes, add the stock and stir until bubbling. Simmer for 20-30 minutes, and then check seasoning.

- You can serve at this stage, adding a hint of brandy to the soup before serving.

- Option – Slice the bread, and toast one side. Spread mustard on un-toasted side and sprinkle on cheese. Brown under the grill, and place a slice on each bowl of soup before serving.

soups

Tomato & Red Pepper Soup

Time to prepare: 5 minutes
Time to cook: 20 minutes

Serves 4

8 medium-size tomatoes
50g (2oz) butter
1 medium-size onion, finely chopped
1 red pepper – chopped
450 ml (15fl.oz) chicken stock (vegetable if vegetarian)
1 pinch saffron
1 pinch chilli powder
Salt
Fresh parsley, if desired

- Put the tomatoes into a bowl and cover with boiling water for 1 minute and then drain. Cover with cold water for 1 minute then drain again. Remove and discard the skins and chop the tomatoes.

- In a large saucepan, melt the butter then add the onion. Cook until it begins to soften. Add the tomatoes, chopped red pepper, stock and saffron. Bring to a boil then reduce the heat.

- Cover & simmer for about ten minutes, then stir in the chilli powder and salt to taste. Garnish with parsley, if desired.

soups

Starters & snacks

Stilton & Walnut Salad

Time to prepare: 15 minutes

Serves 4

2 tablespoons extra virgin olive oil
2 tablespoons walnut oil
1 tablespoon white wine vinegar
For the salad:
100g (3½oz) mixed baby leaf salad
250g (8½oz) stilton, sliced
12 croutons
50g (1¾oz) of walnuts, chopped

- Mix together the extra virgin and walnut oils with the white wine vinegar and set aside.

- Place the salad mixture in a large bowl and pour over the dressing, mix thoroughly.

- To serve, divide the salad between four plates, place a few slices of stilton on top and scatter the croutons and walnuts.

starters & snacks

Easy-peasy Spanish Omelette

Time to prepare: 2 minutes
Time to cook: 16 minutes

Serves 2

2 tablespoons olive oil
1 onion, thinly sliced
350g (12oz) potatoes, diced
1 red bell pepper, thinly sliced
1 green bell pepper, thinly sliced
6 eggs, beaten
1 tablespoon chopped fresh parsley
Salt
Freshly ground pepper

- Heat oil in a shallow flameproof casserole dish. Add onion and potatoes and cook, stirring occasionally, 6 to 8 minutes, or until potatoes are tender.

- Stir in bell peppers and cook 2 or 3 minutes.

- Beat together eggs, parsley, salt and pepper and pour into dish. Cook over a low heat for 3 or 4 minutes, or until the eggs have set on the bottom.

- Preheat grill then put the omelette under and cook for 5 or 6 minutes, or until eggs have set. Cut into wedges and serve hot or cold.

starters & snacks

Pizza or Omelette!

Time to prepare – 3 minutes   *Serves 1*
Time to cook – 6 minutes

3 eggs
1 teaspoon Butter
1 plum tomato, thinly sliced
1 teaspoon basil, fresh, chopped
2 tablespoons Italian-style sausage, cooked and cubed
60g (2oz) Mozzarella, grated

- Pre-heat the grill.

- Melt the butter in a small non-stick frying pan. Lightly beat the eggs and add to the frying pan. Move eggs frequently until firm. Turn omelette over and remove from the heat.

- Top with the tomatoes, basil, sausage, and cheese.

- Place under grill until cheese has melted. Serve immediately.

starters & snacks

Brie & Spiced Pear Tartlets

Time to prepare – 10 minutes   *Serves 4*
Time to cook – 15-20 minutes

80g (3oz) butter
200g (7oz) pack filo pastry
1 can pears in natural juice, drained, dried and chopped
300g (10½oz) firm Brie
Half a teaspoon allspice
1 tablespoon chopped fresh chives

- Pre-heat oven to 200°C/400°F/gas 6 with a flat baking sheet inside (this helps to crisp the base of the tarts).

- Melt butter over a gentle heat, place one sheet of filo pastry onto a board and brush both sides of the filo with butter. Fold over until you have a 75mm (3″) square, and then push into one of the cups of a Yorkshire pudding tin, tucking the edges inside so that you have a round tart. Repeat with the other sheets, brushing each side with butter as you go.

- Fill each pastry case with an equal amount of pear, brie and a pinch of allspice.

- Stand on a pre-heated baking sheet and bake for 15–20 minutes until golden.

- Scatter with chives just before serving.

King Prawns with Tarragon Sauce

Time to prepare: 5 minutes

Serves 4

Time to cook: 6 minters

50g (1¾oz) butter
1 tablespoon finely chopped garlic
1 tablespoon finely chopped shallots
24 uncooked king prawns
2 tablespoons Pernod
125ml (5fl.oz) double cream
1 tablespoon finely chopped tarragon
Salt and pepper
4 sprigs tarragon

- In a large sauté pan, heat the butter over medium-high heat. Add the garlic, shallots, and prawns, and cook for 2 minutes.

- Remove the pan from the heat and add the Pernod. Return the pan to the heat and carefully flambé.

- Add the cream and tarragon and season with salt and pepper. Cook for 2 more minutes to reduce slightly.

- Garnish each serving with a tarragon leaf.

Creamy Wild Mushrooms

Time to prepare: 3 minutes
Time to cook: 6 minutes

Serves 2

75g (2½oz) butter
Clove of garlic, peeled and finely chopped
350g (12oz) assorted wild mushrooms
A splash of white wine
A little double cream
1 tablespoon of freshly chopped parsley
2 teaspoons of freshly chopped chives
Salt and pepper to taste
2 thick slices of granary bread

- Melt the butter in a frying pan and then add the garlic. Cook gently for about 30 seconds and then add the mushrooms.
- Fry gently for about 3–4 minutes. Then add the wine to the pan and cook for a minute.
- Then put the double cream and herbs into the pan and simmer gently. Check seasoning.
- Toast the bread and place onto the serving plates, top with the mushrooms and a little fresh parsley.

starters & snacks

Main courses

Halibut with a Rich Orange Sauce

Time to prepare: 5 minutes
Time to cook: 20 minutes

Serves 2

60g (2oz) plain flour
½ teaspoon freshly grated nutmeg
2 halibut steaks, about 170g (6oz) each
30g (1oz) butter
6 spring onions, sliced
175ml (6fl.oz) fresh orange juice
1 tablespoon Worcestershire sauce
Juice of ½ lemon
Salt and freshly ground black pepper – to taste

- Mix together flour and nutmeg and use to coat halibut.

- Heat butter in a shallow frying pan. Add the spring onions to the pan and cook gently, stirring occasionally for 3 minutes, or until soft.

- Add the halibut and cook over a low heat for 5 to 6 minutes on each side until just cooked. Remove from the pan with a fish slice and keep warm.

- Into the pan put the orange juice, Worcestershire sauce, lemon juice, salt and pepper and boil rapidly until reduced and thickened.

- Pour over fish and serve.

main courses

Baked Cod Italienne

Time to prepare: 5 minutes
Time to cook: 35 minutes

Serves 4

30g (1oz) butter
125g (4½oz) sliced mushrooms
1 jar passata
4 cod steaks, about 155g (5½oz) each or other white fish
Salt and freshly ground pepper
125g (4oz) pasta shells
8 black olives

- Preheat oven to 190C/375°F/gas 5. In a medium-size saucepan, melt butter. Add mushrooms; cook gently until soft. Stir in the passata.

- Put fish into a buttered 2-quart oblong baking dish. Season with salt and pepper.

- Pour tomato and mushroom sauce over fish. Cover dish with foil; bake about 25 minutes or until fish is opaque when tested with a fork.

- Meanwhile, cook pasta until just tender to the bite.

- About 5 minutes before fish has finished cooking, arrange pasta around fish, spooning some of sauce over pasta. Garnish with olives and serve.

main courses

Duck with Apples & Prunes

Time to prepare: 5 minutes
Time to cook: 75 minutes

Serves 4

1 tablespoon olive oil
4 boneless duck breasts, 113g (4oz) each
2 cooking apples, peeled, cored, sliced
225g (8oz) pitted prunes
550ml (18fl.oz) unsweetened apple juice
Salt and freshly ground black pepper

- Preheat oven to 200°C/400°F/gas 6.
- Heat oil in a shallow flameproof casserole dish, add duck and cook 3 or 4 minutes on each side, until browned.
- Cover with the apple slices and prunes. Pour apple juice over duck and season with salt and pepper. Bring to a boil, cover with a lid or piece of foil and bake 55–60 minutes, or until duck is cooked through.
- Remove duck from dish with a slotted spoon, leaving behind apples and prunes, and keep warm.
- Bring cooking juices in dish to a boil and boil 5 minutes, or until liquid has reduced and thickened. Pour the sauce, apples and prunes over duck and serve.

main courses

Garlic Roasted Chicken

Time to prepare: 5 minutes
Time to cook: 60 minutes

Serves 4

2 tablespoons olive oil
6 cloves garlic, thinly sliced
8 chicken thighs
113g (4oz) fennel, cut into wide strips
1 carrot, cut into wide strips
1 parsnip, cut into wide strips
1 large potato, diced
1 red bell pepper, diced
1 green bell pepper, chopped

- Preheat oven to 220°C/425°F/gas 7.

- On the hob, heat the oil in a shallow flameproof dish.
  Add the garlic and cook 2 or 3 minutes.

- Place the chicken and vegetables into the pan and turn
  to coat in the garlic oil.

- Put the lid on the casserole and bake for 55 or 60 minutes,
  or until juices are clear when chicken is pierced with a fork.
  Serve hot.

Chicken on the Vine

Time to prepare: 5 minutes
Time to cook: 20 minutes

Serves 4

4 chicken breasts – halved, boned, and skinned
Salt and freshly grated nutmeg, as needed
2 tablespoons butter or margarine
1 tablespoon orange marmalade
¼ teaspoon dried tarragon
2 spring onions, thinly sliced (use part of the green)
80ml (2½fl.oz) dry white wine
100g (3½oz) seedless grapes
125ml (5fl.oz) whipping cream

- Sprinkle chicken breasts with salt and nutmeg.

- In a large frying pan, heat butter over medium-high heat and brown chicken lightly.

- Add marmalade, tarragon, spring onion, and wine. Cover, reduce heat, and simmer 10 minutes.

- Add grapes, cover again, and continue cooking until chicken is cooked through (about 10 minutes longer; test in the thickest part with a small kitchen knife).

- Using a slotted spoon, remove the chicken and grapes to a heated serving dish; keep warm.

- Add the cream to the liquid in season to taste. Pour sauce over chicken and serve.

Chicken Livers with Mango

Time to prepare: 5 minutes
Time to cook: 12 minutes

Serves 4

1 tablespoon olive oil
1 small onion, chopped
340g (12oz) chicken livers, trimmed
300ml (10fl.oz) low-fat fromage frais
2 teaspoons Worcestershire sauce
2 teaspoons whole-grain mustard
1 mango, sliced
Basil sprigs, to garnish

- Heat the oil in a flameproof casserole dish. Add onion and cook, stirring occasionally, 5 minutes, or until soft.

- Add chicken livers and cook, stirring, 5 minutes.

- In a small bowl, mix together fromage frais or sour cream, Worcestershire sauce and mustard. Add to chicken livers in dish.

- Add mango slices and cook over low heat, stirring, 2 minutes. Garnish with basil sprigs and serve immediately.

main courses

Turkey Milanese

Time to prepare: 5 minutes
Time to cook: 50 minutes

Serves 4

1 egg, beaten
113g (4oz) fresh white breadcrumbs
Grated rind of 1 lemon
Juice of 1 lemon
Salt and freshly ground black pepper
4 turkey breast fillets (113g/4oz each),
   pounded until thin
30g (1oz) butter
2 tablespoons olive oil
340g (12oz) courgettes, sliced
2 teaspoons chopped fresh tarragon
Lemon wedges, to serve

- Preheat oven to 200°C/400°F/gas 6.

- Place egg in a shallow bowl. Mix together breadcrumbs,
  lemon rind, salt and pepper and put on a large plate.
  Dip turkey in egg and then bread crumbs.

- Heat butter and oil in a shallow flameproof casserole dish.
  Add the turkey and cook 3 minutes on each side, until crisp
  and golden.

- Add courgettes and tarragon. Sprinkle with lemon juice
  and season with pepper. Cover and bake for 35 to
  40 minutes. Serve with lemon wedges.

The Big Chef's Hot Pot

Time to prepare: 10 minutes   *Serves 4*
Time to cook: 2 hours, but the longer the better

450g (1lb) middle or best end lamb
Salt and Pepper to taste
2 carrots
1 small turnip
1 small swede
2 sliced leeks
900g (2lb) peeled and sliced potatoes
2 lamb stock cubes made up in ½ litre (1pt) water
A little beef dripping

- Cut meat into neat pieces and dust with pepper and salt.
- Put a layer of sliced potatoes on the bottom of a casserole dish.
- Then place alternate layers of meat and vegetables a bit like making a lasagne.
- Add extra seasonings if wanted. Finish with a layer of thickly sliced potatoes, overlapping. Pour in about ½ litre (1pt) of lamb stock – sufficient to come about one-third of the way up the casserole – and cover the top of the potatoes with little dabs of dripping.
- Cover casserole and put into a fairly low oven for about 2 hours. For the last half an hour uncover the casserole, raise the oven to 180°C/350°F/gas 4 and brown the top layer of potatoes.

main courses

Braised Beef in Guinness

Time to prepare: 10 minutes
Time to cook: 2 hours

Serves 4

60g (2oz) plain flour
Salt and freshly ground pepper
900g (2lb) of lean braising steak, trimmed and sliced thickly
4 tablespoons vegetable oil
3 large onions, sliced
1 tablespoon of brown sugar
600ml (1pt) Guinness
Bouquet Garni sachet

- Season the flour with salt and pepper and toss the meat in the mixture to coat.
- Heat the oil in a large heavy pan and brown the meat in batches, and then set aside.
- Gently fry the onions in the same pan until soft, and then de-glaze the bottom of the pan with the Guinness and the sugar.
- Add the meat and bouquet garni. Bring to the boil. Reduce the heat, cover and cook very gently for about 2 hours until the meat is tender.
- Remove bouquet garni just before serving.

main courses

Toad in the Hole

Time to prepare: 5 minutes
Time to cook: 45 minutes

Serves 4

113g (4oz) plain flour
1 pinch salt
1 teaspoon mixed dried herbs
1 egg, beaten
300ml (10fl.oz) milk
1 tablespoon sunflower oil
1 small onion, chopped
450g (1lb) sausages

- Preheat oven to 200°C/400°F/gas 6.

- In a large bowl, mix together flour, salt and herbs. Make a well in centre and add egg and half of the milk. Beat to a smooth batter. Stir in remaining milk and mix until smooth.

- Heat the oil in a shallow flameproof casserole dish. Add onion and cook, stirring occasionally, for about 3 minutes.

- Add sausages and cook until browned and cooked through. Drain off excess fat.

- Pour batter into dish and bake 30 minutes, or until batter is risen and golden. Serve immediately.

Variation: There are many types of sausages available. Try using different types to vary this recipe.

main courses

Leek & Cheese Tart

v

Time to prepare: 10 minutes
Time to cook: 30 minutes

Serves 4

8 slim prepared leeks
Salt and black pepper
226g (8oz) ready made puff pastry
1 tablespoon French coarse grain mustard
1 egg
60g (2oz) Lancashire cheese

- Pre heat the oven to 230°C/450°F/gas 8

- Arrange the leeks in a frying pan, cover with water, add a pinch of salt and bring to the boil. Reduce the heat and simmer for about 6 minutes.

- While they are cooking, roll out the pastry to a 25cm (10") square and then put the pastry square onto a baking sheet. Cut a groove into the pastry about half an inch in from the outside edges.

- Drain the leeks and cool them under cold running water and then allow to dry. Put the leeks inside the groove of the pastry case and brush them with the mustard.

- Break the egg and beat it lightly and then brush around the outside edge of the tart. Grate the cheese and spread over the top of the leeks.

- Bake in the oven for about 15 minutes or until the pastry has risen and the cheese has melted. Serve hot or warm.

Steak with mash & onion marmalade

Time to prepare: 10 minutes
Time to cook: 30 minutes

Serves 4

900g (2lb) King Edward potatoes
125 ml (5fl.oz) olive oil
2 sprigs of rosemary
4 tablespoons chopped fresh parsley
3 onions, thinly sliced
2 garlic cloves, crushed
2 tablespoons red wine vinegar
60g (2oz) butter
3 tablespoons milk
A little nutmeg
4 x 175g (6oz) fillet steaks

- Cut the potatoes into chunks and put into a pan of cold salted water and cook until tender.

- Meanwhile put 75ml (2.½fl.oz) olive oil and the rosemary into a small pan and gently heat and then set aside for 15 minutes.

- Remove the rosemary and discard. Add half the parsley and blitz with a hand blender or food processor and set aside.

- Heat the remaining oil in a frying pan, add the onions, garlic and cook over a low heat for about 20 minutes until softened.

- Add a pinch of sugar and the vinegar and cook for 7 minutes. Season to taste, remove from the heat and keep warm.

main courses

- Drain the potatoes and then put back into the pan along with the butter, milk and nutmeg. Stir and add remaining parsley. Set aside and keep warm.

- Heat a griddle pan until hot then cook the steaks for 4 minutes each side for medium.

- To serve, make a small mound of potato in the centre of each plate, place the steak on top and a spoon of onion marmalade on top of the steak. Drizzle the rosemary oil around the potato and serve.

main courses

Oriental-Style Stuffed Peppers

Time to prepare: 5 minutes
Time to cook: 60minutes

Serves 4

The flavours of the Orient go well with baked peppers.

4 green or red bell peppers
175g (6oz) cooked white rice
2 teaspoons oil
¼ cup onion, minced
1 teaspoon ginger, fresh, peeled and minced
1 teaspoon garlic, minced
3 tablespoons soy sauce
1 tablespoon sherry
225ml (7½fl.oz) beef stock

- Cut the tops off the peppers. Remove the inner membrane. Drop into boiling water for 3 minutes. Drain.

- Heat the oil in a small frying pan. Add the onion, ginger and garlic. Cook for 2 minutes, stirring frequently.

- In a large bowl mix the rice, onion, ginger, garlic, soy sauce, sherry and stock. Add the mixture to the peppers.

- Stand the peppers up in a deep casserole dish. Cover with foil and bake at 180C/350°F/gas 4 for 45 minutes.

- Remove the foil and bake for 15 minutes longer. Serve whilst hot.

main courses

Stilton & Sage Farfalle

Time to prepare: 5 minutes
Time to cook: 12 minutes

Serves 4

450g (1lb) farfalle – (any pasta that you have will do)
1 garlic clove, crushed
150ml (5fl.oz) dry white wine
175g (6oz) of stilton, crumbled
4 tablespoons thick plain Greek yoghurt
4 fresh sage leaves, chopped
4 tablespoons freshly grated parmesan
Salt and freshly ground pepper to taste

- Cook the pasta in boiling salted water for about 10 minutes or until al dente (slightly underdone).

- In a small saucepan, mix together the garlic and wine and cook over a high heat for 1 minute. Turn down the heat; add the stilton, Greek yoghurt and sage to the pan. Heat gently, stirring constantly, until the cheese begins to melt.

- Drain the pasta and transfer to a warm serving bowl, pour the sauce over and toss thoroughly to combine.

- Sprinkle the parmesan on top, a little seasoning and serve.

main courses

Vegetable & side dishes

Ye Olde Bubble & Squeak

Time to prepare: 5 minutes
Time to cook: 20 minutes

Serves 4

This classic dish originally contained beef along with the left-over cooked potatoes and cabbage, though today people don't generally bother with the meat. The name is apparently due to the sounds that are emitted during cooking, the vegetables bubble as they are boiled and then squeak in the frying pan.

30g (½oz) Butter
1 onion, finely chopped
450g (1lb) potatoes, cooked and mashed
225g (8oz) cabbage, finely chopped and cooked
6 slices beef, cooked and finely chopped

- Melt the butter in a large frying pan; add the onion and fry for a few minutes until softened, stirring frequently.
- Add the potatoes and cabbage. If you are including the beef, add this as well. Fry over a medium heat for 15 minutes until brown then serve.

Serving hint: fabulous for breakfast with chopped bacon instead of beef, with a fried egg on top

Potato Mash with Garlic

Time to prepare: 5 minutes

Serves 4

Time to cook: 25 minutes

450g (1lb) King Edward potatoes,
113g (4oz) celeriac
1 clove garlic, crushed
Freshly ground black pepper
30g (½oz) unsalted butter
30g (½oz) parmesan cheese, freshly grated

- Cut potatoes and celeriac into even-sized chunks and cover in salted water; cook until tender.

- Drain well, then mash smoothly. Beat in the unsalted butter, garlic, pepper and Parmesan.

- Season with salt and pepper to taste; and serve.

vegetable & side dishes

Cheese Scalloped Potatoes

Time to prepare: 5 minutes
Time to cook: 70 minutes

Serves 4

3 large potatoes, medium-thin sliced
113g (4oz) smoked cheese, grated
2 tablespoons onion, minced
1½ teaspoons flour
500ml (1pt) milk
Salt and pepper to taste

- Heat oven to 190C/375°F/gas 5.
- Blanch potato slices in boiling water for 5 minutes. Drain and rinse with cold water.
- Lightly grease a casserole with oil. Make a layer of half of the potatoes. Top with the cheese, onion, and flour. Top with the rest of the potatoes.
- Season the milk slightly, heat and pour over the casserole. Cover and bake for 50 minutes. Uncover and bake for 20 minutes longer (or until lightly brown).
- Serve hot, but delicious cold.

vegetable & side dishes

Creamed Parsnips

Time to prepare: 5 minutes
Time to cook: 30–45 minutes

Serves 4

This smooth purée is an excellent accompaniment to roast meats, poultry and game. This was a popular dish in the 16th and 17th centuries, when food with a sweet flavour, such as parsnips, was often served as a complement to savoury dishes.

More recently I prepared and served this simple dish to Dame Judi Dench as part of a Christmas dinner at my publisher's house. She loved it!

900g (2lbs) parsnips – peeled and roughly chopped
145g (5oz) single cream
Chopped fresh parsley – to garnish

- Cook the parsnips in salted boiling water for 25–40 minutes, until very tender.
- Drain thoroughly then return to the pan and mash, using a potato masher or a food processor.
- Stir in the cream and season to taste. Heat gently, then serve hot, garnished with parsley.

vegetable & side dishes

English Mustard Mash

Time to prepare: 5 minutes
Time to cook: 20 minutes

Serves 4

8 large potatoes, peeled and cut into even chunks
250ml (10fl.oz) full cream milk
75g (2½oz) unsalted butter
4 tablespoons English mustard
Salt and freshly ground pepper to taste

- Put the potatoes into a large saucepan, cover with cold
  salted water and bring to the boil. Simmer gently for
  15 minutes or until tender.

- Remove from the pan and drain. Put the milk and butter into
  the empty pan, heat to melt the butter and bring to the boil.

- Return the potatoes to the pan and mash thoroughly.
  Add the mustard and mix well, season to taste.

Wonderful with sausages for a delicious variation on bangers
& mash!

vegetable & side dishes

Irish-Style Onion Rings

Time to prepare: 5 minutes
Time to cook: 10 minutes

Serves 4

You can use any beer in this recipe, but Guinness works best.

200g (7oz) cream cracker crumbs
½ teaspoon garlic powder
½ teaspoon onion powder
⅛ teaspoon pepper
225ml (10fl.oz) Guinness
1 egg
145g (5oz) flour
2 large onions
Oil for frying

- Preheat the oil to 360°C/680°F/gas ?.
- Mix together the crumbs, garlic powder, onion powder and pepper.
- Lightly beat the egg in a separate bowl. Whisk in the flour and beer.
- Slice the onions into 6mm (¼") rings. Dip the rings first into the batter and then into the crumbs. Add to the hot oil in batches (turning once) and cook in the oil until lightly brown (about 2 minutes).
- Drain on paper towels.

vegetable & side dishes

Puddings

Baked Panettone Pudding

Time to prepare: 5 minutes + 15 minutes soaking *Serves 2*
Time to cook: 50 minutes

2 eggs, beaten
75g (2½oz) sugar
200ml (7fl.oz) whole milk
½ teaspoon vanilla extract
3 slices panettone with dried fruit – or other rich yeast bread
1 tablespoon marmalade
Icing sugar for dusting

- Preheat oven to 165°C/325°F/gas 3.

- In a large bowl, beat eggs and sugar until light and foamy. Add milk and vanilla extract and mix well.

- Lightly butter a shallow ovenproof dish.

- Spread slices of panettone with orange marmalade. Sandwich together, 2 pieces at a time, and cut the pieces in half. Arrange in the dish. Ladle the egg mixture over the panettone and soak 15 minutes.

- Place dish in a larger ovenproof dish or roasting pan and pour in enough boiling water to come halfway up the sides of dish. Bake 50 minutes, or until custard is set and top is golden with a slight crust. Sprinkle with icing sugar and serve hot or cold.

puddings

Flambéed Fruit

Time to prepare: 5 minutes
Time to cook: 10 minutes

Serves 4

60g (2oz) butter
60g (2oz) sugar
2 oranges, peeled, segmented
1 can (340g/12oz) pineapple pieces in natural juice
4 bananas, thickly sliced
1 tablespoon orange liqueur or brandy
Mint sprigs, to garnish

- Put butter and sugar in a flameproof casserole dish and cook over low heat until melted and a caramel colour.

- Add oranges, pineapple chunks and their juice and bananas. Bring to a boil and boil 5 minutes, or until sauce thickens.

- Put liqueur or brandy in a ladle and warm gently. Set alight and pour over fruit. Cook 1 minute, until flames die down. Garnish with mint and serve warm.

puddings

Rhubarb Meringue

Time to prepare: 5 minutes
Time to cook: 40 minutes

Serves 4

450g (1lb) rhubarb, sliced
4 bananas, sliced
60g (2oz) light-brown sugar
5g (1 teaspoon) ground cinnamon
Grated rind of 3 oranges
Juice of 3 oranges
Foe meringue:
3 egg whites
175g (6oz) sugar

- Preheat oven to 180°C/350°F/gas 4.

- Put rhubarb and bananas in an ovenproof dish. Sprinkle with brown sugar, cinnamon and orange rind. Add orange juice, making sure fruit is evenly coated.

- Cover with a lid or piece of foil and bake 15 to 20 minutes, or until fruit is tender.

- Meanwhile, to make meringue, beat egg whites until they form stiff peaks. Beat in sugar.

- Put meringue into a pastry bag with a star tip and pipe over fruit. Return to oven and cook 20 minutes, or until meringue is crisp and golden. Serve warm or cold.

Saucy Lime Pudding

Time to prepare: 5 minutes
Time to cook: 40 – 50 minutes

Serves 4

60g (2oz) unsalted butter, softened
60g (2oz) sugar
Grated rind 3 limes
Juice 3 limes
2 eggs, separated
60g (2oz) self raising flour
300ml (10fl.oz) milk

- Preheat oven to 160°C/325°F/gas 3.

- In a large bowl, beat together butter, sugar and lime rind until light and fluffy. Stir in egg yolks and carefully fold in flour. Stir in milk and lime juice.

- Whisk egg whites until they form stiff peaks. Fold into lime mixture. Lightly butter an ovenproof dish.

- Pour lime mixture into dish and bake 40 to 50 minutes, or until risen and golden. Serve warm.

puddings

Ignorance is Bliss

v

Time to prepare: 5 minutes + chilling

Serves 4

500ml (1pt) whipping cream
A good splash (at least 5ml!) of Baileys, Amarula, Tia Maria, or favourite liqueur
1 Crunchie bar – smashed with a rolling pin whilst still in packet

- Whisk together the cream and liqueur until almost firm then add the Crunchie pieces and whisk for 15 seconds.
- Leave to chill in fridge for 1 hour minimum.

Just the simplest thing to make, but tastes out of this world!

puddings

Mint White Chocolate Mousse

Time to prepare: 10 minutes + chilling   *Serves 4*

113g (4oz) white chocolate
3 tablespoons green Crème de menthe
150ml (5fl.oz) double cream,
2 egg whites (at room temperature)

- Melt the white chocolate in a double boiler, or a glass bowl sat on a pan of boiling water.

- When melted, stir in the crème de menthe. Let it cool a bit and stir in about 2½ tablespoons of cream. Leave to cool.

- Beat the egg whites until stiff, but not dry. Fold the chocolate-crème-cream mixture into the beaten egg whites. The more carefully you fold; the lighter will be the mousse.

- Whip the remaining cream, until soft peaks form. Fold the egg whites-chocolate mixture into the whipped cream. Again, the more air you preserve, the lighter the mousse.

- Spoon carefully into small bowls or cups and chill for about two hours.

- Serve topped with a strawberry.

puddings

Tipsy Fruit Fool

Time to prepare: 5 minutes
Time to cook: 10 minutes + chilling

Serves 4

450g (1lb) cooking apples, peeled, sliced
155g (5½oz) dried apricots, pre-soaked
60g (2oz) icing sugar
Rind of 3 satsumas
Juice of 3 satsumas
30ml (2 tablespoons) apricot brandy
90ml (3fl.oz) fromage frais
Chocolate curls to decorate

- In a saucepan, combine apples, apricots, sugar and satsuma rind and juice. Bring to a boil.

- Cover and cook until apples and apricots are tender. Remove satsuma rind and reserve some for decoration. Let stand until cold.

- In a food processor fitted with a metal blade, process apple mixture to a puree.

- Add apricot brandy and fromage frais and process until well blended. Divide mixture among individual glasses and chill until needed.

- Using a sharp knife, cut reserved rind in thin strips. Decorate desserts with satsuma rind strips and chocolate curls.

Spicy French Toast

Time to prepare: 15 mins
Time to cook: 10 mins

Serves 4

4 slices of white bread
3 large eggs
1 teaspoon grated nutmeg
1 teaspoon cinnamon
A little caster sugar
4 tablespoons of double cream

- Cut the crusts off the bread and cut into triangles, beat the eggs with the grated nutmeg and cinnamon.

- Heat a frying pan with a little oil and butter in it. Dip each piece of bread into the egg mixture and fry until golden brown before turning and cook on the other side.

- To serve put 4 triangles onto each plate, sprinkle with a little cinnamon and caster sugar, and serve warm with a dollop of double cream.

puddings

Banana & Mango Fool

Time to prepare: 5 minutes + chilling *Serves 4*

4 small bananas, peeled and sliced
1 ripe mango, peeled and chopped
Grated zest and juice of one lime
2 tablespoons caster sugar
300ml (10fl.oz) double cream

- Puree the bananas, mango, lime juice and sugar together in a blender.

- Whip the cream until it stands in soft peaks, and then gently fold into the mango mixture a little at a time.

- Put into glass dishes and chill until required.

- When ready to eat, sprinkle with grated lime zest and serve.

puddings

Hot Peaches with honey

Time to prepare: 10 minutes

Time to cook: 5 minutes

Serves 4

4 fresh peaches
100g (3½oz) Mascarpone cheese
3 tablespoons clear honey
2 tablespoons flaked almonds
For the syrup:
200g (7oz) sugar
400ml (13½fl.oz) of water
Half a teaspoon vanilla essence
Juice of half a lemon

- First make the syrup. Gently dissolve the sugar in the water in the pan. Add the essence and lemon juice.

- Half the peaches, remove the stones, add to the syrup and poach for 4 minutes or until soft.

- To serve, fill each peach with Mascarpone, drizzle with honey and sprinkle with flaked almonds.

puddings

Proper Custard!

Time to prepare: 5 minutes
Time to cook: 15 minutes

Serves 4

300ml (10fl.oz) full cream milk
300ml (10fl.oz) double cream
4 egg yolks
2 tablespoons caster sugar
1 vanilla pod, split
1 tablespoon of water
1 tablespoon of cornflour

- Gently warm the cream and milk in a saucepan with the vanilla pod but do not let it boil.

- Beat the egg yolks with the sugar, remove the vanilla pod from the cream mixture and pour slowly onto the eggs, stirring constantly.

- Mix the cornflour with the water and pour into the egg mixture.

- Return the mixture to the saucepan and stir over a low heat until the mixture thickens and coats the back of a spoon (about 10 minutes). Again, do not allow to boil.

- Strain the custard into a bowl and put a piece of damp cling film on the surface to prevent a skin forming and chill.

puddings

Sauces

Béchamel sauce

This sauce is the basis of most white sauces, both sweet and savoury. Follow the recipes to the letter and you will never have lumpy sauces again!

600ml (1pt) milk
1 onion with 2 cloves stuck in
1 carrot (peeled and chopped)
Bouquet garni
60g (2oz) butter
60g (2oz) flour
Salt
Freshly ground black pepper
Freshly grated nutmeg.

- Into a saucepan put the milk, onion, carrot and bouquet garni. Bring slowly to the boil and then reduce the heat to a slow simmer for 30 minutes to infuse.

- In a separate saucepan melt the butter and stir in the flour with a wooden spoon. This is called making a 'roux'. Cook for one minute stirring constantly – this is very important otherwise the finished sauce will have a floury taste.

- Remove the saucepan from the heat and gradually add the milk a little at a time. Stir vigorously all the time. At this stage the sauce should be runny without any lumps.

- Return the pan to the heat and simmer gently for about five minutes until the sauce thickens.

Variations: Add tarragon, parsley etc. to make different sauces.

sauces

Tomato sauce

2 tablespoons olive oil
1 medium onion (finely chopped)
2 crushed cloves garlic
60ml (2fl.oz) red wine
800g (28oz) tinned tomatoes
2 tablespoons tomato ketchup
½ tablespoon dried thyme
½ tablespoon dried basil.

- Heat the oil in a saucepan, add onion and garlic and cook until soft but not coloured.

- Add the wine and simmer until reduced by half.

- Add the rest of the ingredients and simmer for 10 minutes or until thickened.

This recipe can be frozen for storage.

Basic cheese sauce

60g (2oz) butter
60g (2oz) flour
400ml (13½fl.oz) milk
40g (1½oz) mature Cheddar cheese.

- Put the milk into a saucepan, bring slowly to the boil and then reduce the heat to a slow simmer.

- In a separate saucepan melt the butter and stir in the flour with a wooden spoon. This is called making a 'roux'. Cook for about a minute, stirring constantly – this is very important otherwise the finished sauce will have a floury taste.

- Remove the saucepan from the heat and gradually add the milk, a little at a time. Stir vigorously all the time. At this stage the sauce should be runny without any lumps.

- Return the pan to the heat and simmer gently for about five minutes until the sauce thickens.

- Remove from the heat, allow to cool very slightly, and then stir in the cheese.

Velouté sauce

60g (2oz) butter
60g (2oz) flour
500ml (1pt) chicken stock
1 bay leaf
2 sprigs parsley
1 sprig thyme
6 black peppercorns

- In a saucepan melt the butter, stir in the flour and heat for about a minute stirring continuously.
- Remove the saucepan from the heat and gradually add the stock, stirring all the time.
- Add the remainder of the ingredients, and return the pan to the heat. Simmer gently for about 25 minutes.
- Skim any fat from the surface of the sauce during the cooking. Strain sauce through a fine sieve.

Variation: Add a little double cream after the sieving stage for an even richer sauce.

sauces

Vinaigrette

6 tablespoons virgin olive oil
2 tablespoons white wine vinegar
1 teaspoon dark smooth Dijon mustard
Pinch sugar, salt and pepper

- In a glass bowl whisk together the oil and vinegar with a small balloon whisk.
- Whisk in the mustard and sugar until mixed thoroughly.
- Add salt and pepper to taste.

Mint sauce

125ml (4fl.oz) water
75g (2½oz) sugar
250ml (8½fl.oz) cider vinegar
Handful chopped mint

- In a small saucepan heat the water until hot but not boiling, add the sugar and stir to dissolve. Now bring to the boil and boil rapidly for five minutes.
- Remove from the heat, stir in the vinegar and mint, and leave to stand for 10–15 minutes.
- Stir before serving.

sauces

Tarragon & mushroom sauce

30g (1oz) butter
226g (8oz) sliced mushrooms
60ml (2fl.oz) dry white wine
1 tablespoon brandy
300ml (10fl.oz) double cream
2 teaspoons water
1 teaspoon arrowroot
1 tablespoon chopped chives
1 teaspoon tarragon

- In a saucepan melt the butter, then add the mushrooms and stir gently until soft. Add the wine and brandy and simmer gently for about five minutes. In a cup mix together the water and arrowroot and add this to the pan. When the sauce thickens stir in the herbs.

- A great sauce to accompany pasta, beef or pork!

Homemade peanut butter

Making homemade peanut butter is easy when using a food processor. The following makes 1 jar ...

100g (3½oz) peanuts (shelled and unsalted)
1½ tablespoons vegetable oil
Salt to taste

- Pulse the peanuts in the processor until smooth (about one minute).
- With the machine running, slowly add the oil and run until smooth.
- Check the seasoning. Store covered in the refrigerator.

The qualities of an exceptional cook are akin to those of a successful tightrope walker: an abiding passion for the task, courage to go out on a limb and an impeccable sense of balance.

Bryan Millert

My tips

Index

'The Greatest Tips in the World' books

Baby & Toddler Tips
by Vicky Burford
ISBN 978-1-905151-70-7

Barbeque Tips
by Raymond van Rijk
ISBN 978-1-905151-68-4

Cat Tips by Joe Inglis
ISBN 978-1-905151-66-0

Cookery Tips
by Peter Osborne
ISBN 978-1-905151-64-6

Cricketing Tips
by R. Rotherham & G. Clifford
ISBN 978-1-905151-18-9

DIY Tips
by Chris Jones & Brian Lee
ISBN 978-1-905151-62-2

Dog Tips by Joe Inglis
ISBN 978-1-905151-67-7

Etiquette & Dining Tips
by Prof. R. Rotherham
ISBN 978-1-905151-21-9

Freelance Writing Tips
by Linda Jones
ISBN 978-1-905151-17-2

Gardening Tips
by Steve Brookes
ISBN 978-1-905151-60-8

Genealogy Tips
by M. Vincent-Northam
ISBN 978-1-905151-72-1

Golfing Tips
by John Cook
ISBN 978-1-905151-63-9

Horse & Pony Tips
by Joanne Bednall
ISBN 978-1-905151-19-6

Household Tips
by Vicky Burford
ISBN 978-1-905151-61-5

Personal Success Tips
by Brian Larcher
ISBN 978-1-905151-71-4

Podcasting Tips
by Malcolm Boyden
ISBN 978-1-905151-75-2

Property Developing Tips
by F. Morgan & P Morgan
ISBN 978-1-905151-69-1

Retirement Tips
by Tony Rossiter
ISBN 978-1-905151-28-8

Sex Tips
by Julie Peasgood
ISBN 978-1-905151-74-5

Travel Tips
by Simon Worsfold
ISBN 978-1-905151-73-8

Yoga Tips
by D. Gellineau & D. Robson
ISBN 978-1-905151-65-3

Pet Recipe books

The Greatest Feline Feasts in the World by Joe Inglis
ISBN 978-1-905151-50-9

The Greatest Doggie Dinners in the World by Joe Inglis
ISBN 978-1-905151-51-6

'The Greatest in the World' DVDs

The Greatest in the World – Gardening Tips
presented by Steve Brookes

The Greatest in the World – Yoga Tips
presented by David Gellineau and David Robson

The Greatest in the World – Cat & Kitten Tips
presented by Joe Inglis

The Greatest in the World – Dog & Puppy Tips
presented by Joe Inglis

For more information about currently available
and forthcoming book and DVD titles please visit:

www.thegreatestintheworld.com

The GREATEST
in the WORLD

or write to:

The Greatest in the World Ltd
PO Box 3182
Stratford-upon-Avon
Warwickshire CV37 7XW
United Kingdom

Tel / Fax: +44(0)1789 299616
Email: info@thegreatestintheworld.com

The author

Peter Osborne, 'The Big Chef', is one of the most accomplished cookery presenters around with an exceptional ability to communicate his passion for cooking in a lively and fun way. For the past 5 years he has performed his live cookery show all over Britain and Europe.

Peter's TV credits include Granada TV, Breeze & Carlton Food Network, BBC Breakfast and This Morning, as well as air time on European and USA networks. He has a regular cookery spot on The Graham Rogers Show at Classic Gold Radio.

In addition to broadcast work Peter regularly contributes to a variety of publications where his recipes and columns entertain and inform with his frank yet witty trademark style. The recipes in this book are just a small selection from his first book, Happy Cooking!, which is available to buy online at www.thebigchefcookshop.com.